W9-AEN-172

TIMBERFRAME

The Art and Craft of the Post-and-Beam Home

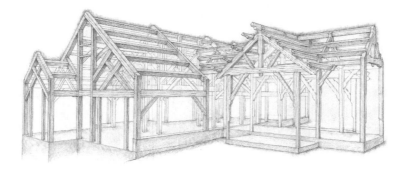

3 1571 00184 1116

TIMBERFRAME

The Art and Craft of the Post-and-Beam Home

TEDD BENSON

Foreword by Norm Abram

GLEN COVE PUBLIC LIBRARY
4 GLEN COVE AVENUE
GLEN COVE. NEW YORK 11542-2885

The Taunton Press

Publisher
Jim Childs

Acquisitions Editor
Steve Culpepper

Editorial Assistant
Carol Kasper

Copy Editor
Peter Chapman

Jacket and Interior Design
Carol Singer

Photographer (except where noted)
James R. Salomon

Illustrator
Kathy Bray

Taunton
BOOKS & VIDEOS
for fellow enthusiasts

Text © 1999 by Tedd Benson
Photos © 1999 by The Taunton Press Inc., except where noted
Illustrations © 1999 by The Taunton Press Inc.
All rights reserved.

Printed in the United States of America
10 9 8 7 6 5 4 3 2 1

The Taunton Press, 63 South Main Street, PO Box 5506, Newtown, CT 06470-5506
e-mail: tp@taunton.com

Distributed by Publishers Group West

FRONTISPIECE PHOTO
Tedd Benson

DEDICATION PHOTO
Bill Holtz

Library of Congress Cataloging-in Publication Data

Benson, Tedd.
    Timberframe : the art and craft of the post-and-beam
home / Tedd Benson; foreword by Norm Abram.
        p. cm.
    ISBN 1-56158-281-6
        1. Wooden-frame houses—Design and construction.   I. Title.
TH4818.W6B46523   1999
728'.37—dc21   99-31212
                                                                      CIP

In memory of my father,
Ted M. Benson
(1910–1997)

Contents

Foreword   2
NORM ABRAM

Prologue: The Art and Craft of the Timberframe   4

Ah, to build, to build! That is the noblest of all the arts.

—Henry Wadsworth Longfellow

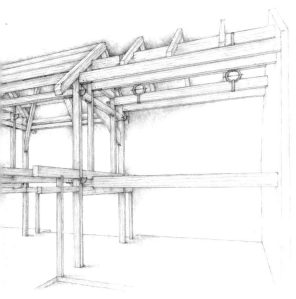

Foreword

Nothing in homebuilding is more dramatic than raising a timberframe. I've watched Tedd Benson oversee the process done the old-fashioned way with lots of people pulling on ropes and pushing with poles as a timberframe that had been assembled on the deck was raised into place section by section, and fastened with joints cut into the wood.

When Tedd and a crew from his shop in New Hampshire erected the timberframe of the ell in my own new house almost five years ago, however, the process didn't look very much like the Amish do it. True, Tedd's crew of five, joined by two carpenters I brought along to assist us, completed the structure in one day. But there were no ropes to be pulled, no crowd watching. The frame was literally more lowered than raised, as a large portable crane lifted great trusses and other members of the frame from a huge logging truck, swung them through the cold November air, and lowered them gently into place. The trusses looked like huge birds gliding through space toward a landing. I still have a photograph of Kurt Doolittle, the lead framer for the project, balancing on one leg on the ridge beam, arms extended like a gymnast, a happy grin plastered on his face.

The frame itself was a fascinating medley of things old and new. The concept of the frame and the nature of the joinery were old. Dimitri Gerakaris had heated the metal for the stirrup braces holding the bottom chords to the king posts on a traditional coal-fired forge and shaped them by hand on an anvil with a 1916-vintage power hammer, but if the job had called for it, he would have cut steel with a plasma cutter. The computer engineering used to design the frame and calculate its weightbearing capacity was new, as were the power tools used to shape and finish the various members and the high-tech glues used to bond the laminated layers of the bottom chords together.

I had selected a truss design in which the horizontal member is slightly arched. The best way to make such an arch is to cut a large beam (Sitka spruce in this case) lengthwise into inch-thick slices, slather epoxy on all the surfaces to be laminated, and then clamp the laminated chord against a curved form until the epoxy is fully set. The spruce was springy enough in its thin slices that it didn't need to be steamed to be flexible enough to bend to the form. Tedd invited me to help laminate one of the bottom chords, so I drove up to New Hampshire just before Halloween that year and joined the crew. I've done a lot of gluing and clamping in my woodworking, but nothing on that scale before!

Almost all of the framing I've done myself has been the construction of skeletons that, however well crafted, were destined to be covered over with exterior siding and roofing and interior finishes. But timberframes are those wonderful exceptions in which the frame is meant to be seen and admired as a finished surface and an architectural element.

In the five years that the timberframe ell has sheltered the open kitchen, family room, and family dining room in my house, the Sitka spruce of the trusses and the Port Orford cedar of the posts and plate beams have darkened slightly under their citrus-based oil finish to a honey brown. The oak pegs and cherry splines make a pleasing variation of color in the woods. The joinery fully deserves the accolade the designer, Bill Holtz, gave it: "a celebration." I gravitate to that part of the house whenever I can because I take so much pleasure in studying the frame. I look at its sturdiness and know it will be standing for many decades, maybe a century or two. In our part of the country, that's what one wants in a home: a sense of durability.

Norm Abram
Boston, Massachusetts
May, 1999

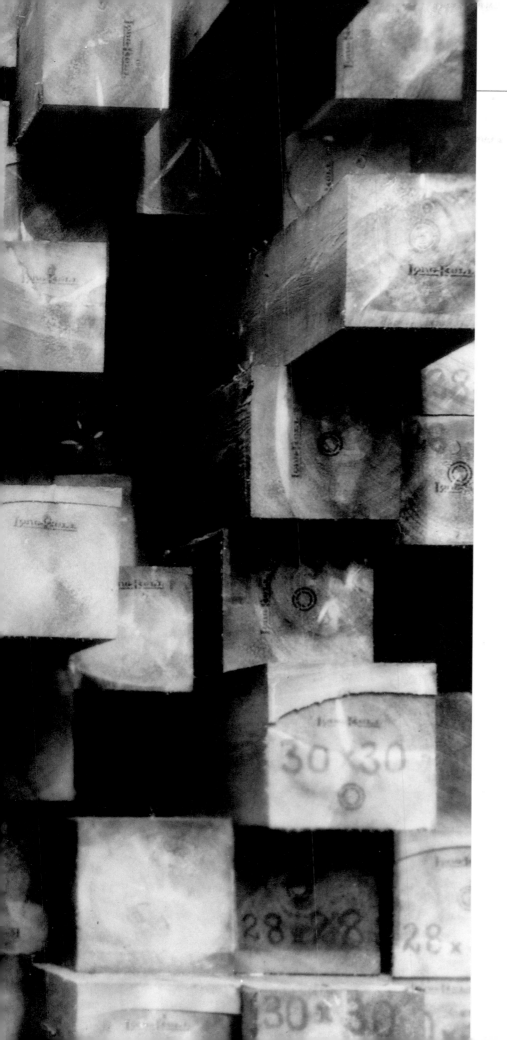

Prologue:
The Art and Craft
of the Timberframe

The strength of a nation

is derived from the

integrity of its homes.

—Confucius

left The Long-Bell mill produced these incredible lumber cants
in the early 1900s, but it was the salvaged timbers
from the dismantled mill itself that contributed to many
modern timberframe homes.

(PHOTO COURTESY LONGVIEW PUBLIC LIBRARY, LONGVIEW ROOM COLLECTION)

Today's timberframe homes are historical and contemporary, relevant and vigorous. Flexible in design and inherently beautiful, they give evidence to the fact that the centuries-old craft of timberframing has returned as a practical and environmentally sensitive building technique.

The timberframe renaissance in North America began with a small group of New England craftsmen in the early 1970s and spread rapidly throughout the continent. Today, timberframing is practiced in nearly every part of North America, and there are hundreds of professional companies making thousands of homes annually. It has been a fortuitous confluence of awakened desires: builders who want work that is more interesting, challenging, and rewarding and owners who aspire to have homes that truly enrich their lives through the structure's art and craft.

A modern timberframe is like a large piece of furniture, intended to be both visible and appreciated. One of the most appealing aspects of the modern timberframe home is the quality and variety of its spaces. Because all of the space within is opened to the living area, timberframes tend to provide more volume per square foot, which makes small spaces feel larger and large spaces more dramatic.

Timberframe homes easily adapt to different regional requirements, climates, and architectural influences. Unlike log buildings, timberframe homes don't all look alike. From coast to coast, from mountains to lakes to prairies, regional and stylistic differences are clear. Timberframing does not dictate the building shape or design and imposes no limitations regarding exterior finishes. Timberframing can be used to build a shingle-style seaside retreat or a rugged stone-and-wood, high-mountain lodge. The design style can be elaborate and formal or simple and rustic. What is constant is the crafted integrity of the timberframe.

While the exterior can be designed to fit public requirements or expectations, the interior is always a unique and personalized work of art. Interior spaces can be open, airy, and light-filled or cozy interior chambers made more comfortable by the warmth of the timbers. The timbers themselves can be highly polished or

The Guildhall of Corpus Christi in Lavenham, England, was built in 1520. Some of the most sophisticated timberframes of all time were produced during this era.

Salvaged fir timbers join to a huge cedar log in a recently built timberframe home.

automatically provides openings between the widely spaced posts and beams that make the installation of doors, windows, or fixed glass a simple proposition. In timberframe building, the spaces between the timbers are literally framed openings, which can be used in a variety of ways without compromising the strength of the structure.

Timberframe homes are sustainable. They use forest resources wisely. In fact, most of the timberframes featured here were built with timbers salvaged from dismantled buildings, and all have the potential to last 300 to 600 years, or the time it takes trees to reach full maturity. Timberframe structures survive because of their rugged strength, but also because the frames are open skeletons that allow extensive flexibility and long-term adaptability. Additionally, because the timberframe is separated from its insulating skin, timberframe homes are among the most energy-efficient available. For these reasons and more, though it is an ancient building form, timberframing is now thoroughly progressive and has carved a solid niche in mainstream homebuilding.

left with a rough-textured, natural finish. With timberframing, there is always a rich palette of design and decoration possibilities, depending on the finishes, the species, and the sculptural arrangement of the framework.

Like the frame itself, today's timberframe home encompasses influences from around the world. You won't see reproductions of homes from Japan, Germany, or England in this book, but you will see the clear influence of these international forms. For the most part, however, the homes featured here evolved most directly from the English medieval building form. This is the dominant tradition in North American timberframe design, and you'll see the "great hall" look—in a variety of styles, shapes, and finishes—repeated throughout.

But the timberframe halls of today are far from medieval. Besides their extremely effective insulation, the biggest difference is light. Unlike other forms of residential construction, timberframing

A LOOK BACK

Timberframing is as old as our concept of home. A self-supporting framework of timbers fastened with wooden connections, timberframing began with the first mortise-and-tenon joint, somewhere between 500 B.C. and 200 B.C. Shaping and joining timbers proved to be a building system so primal and basic that it found its way into forest cultures all around the world.

This recently built southwest Colorado timberframe was constructed primarily with timbers from dismantled mill buildings.

Even when the useful life of a timberframe building is over, it is still possible to salvage and reuse the timbers. In timberframing, the very best material available is often that which can be salvaged from old timber buildings. Using recycled timbers has the inherent benefit of preserving living trees, but the wood is also generally better than that cut from the faster-growing trees of today.

Most of the timberframe homes featured in this book were built with timbers salvaged from other timber structures. And when these houses are dismantled—hopefully at least 500 years in the future—there is no reason the same timbers can't be used again. This unique attribute is satisfying to the owners' ecological conscience, while it also gives the homes added character and an interesting history from the outset.

Whether from old factories, defunct mill buildings, or old barns, the beauty of the wood is enhanced by its history. In this book, some of these histories derive from a Great Salt Lake railroad trestle, a Royal typewriter factory, a Vlasic Pickle factory, an old Massachusetts bridge, and 200-year-old barns. In at least one case, the recycled timbers were from a 19th-century structure that had recycled some of its timbers from an even earlier building.

LONG-BELL'S GIFT

One particular recycling story deserves to be told in full. Nearly two-thirds of the timberframe homes presented in this book share a unique history: Many or all of the timbers in their frames were salvaged from the demolition of a single facility—the Long-Bell Lumber mill complex in Longview, Washington.

In 1918, Robert A. Long, President of the Long-Bell Lumber Company, had a problem: His southern timber holdings were nearly depleted. He would

Located in farm country north of Baltimore, this home's timberframe was built with Douglas fir timbers salvaged from the demolition of the Long-Bell mill buildings in Longview, Washington.

Southern pine timbers salvaged from mill buildings and factories on the East Coast live on in this Nebraska home.

When the Long-Bell mill buildings were built, they were harvesting timbers from the virgin forests in the Longview, Washington, area. Wood from those magnificent trees was also used to build the huge industrial facility. (LONGVIEW PUBLIC LIBRARY, LONGVIEW ROOM COLLECTION)

either have to liquidate his sizeable logging operations and concentrate on his line of hardware stores and retail lumberyards or find another source of timber. Less than a year later, Long and a small crew went on a horseback exploration of the virgin forests in the foothills of the Cascade Mountains in southwestern Washington (where it is estimated that the trees averaged 9 ft. in diameter and 150 ft. in height!).

What Long saw on that expedition must have been breathtaking, even for a man who had spent a lifetime logging the ancient forests. These forests inspired a massive plan that included the design and construction of a city to house the people who would cut the forest down. In the next few years, the Long-

Bell Lumber Company purchased 70,000 acres that contained approximately 3.8 billion board feet of virgin northwestern timber.

As Long's plans for his new Long-Bell mill grew, it became apparent that he would need more than 14,000 workers at the site. He realized it would take a mighty appealing hook to bring that many people to the yet-unsettled outpost. So he hired George Kessler, who was already known for his plans of Kansas City, Dallas, Oklahoma City, Mexico City and the 1904 St. Louis Exposition, to help design a city for 50,000.

Construction of the mill complex and the town began in 1922 and was substantially completed in four to five years. The mill itself was in production by 1924, but didn't reach full capacity until 1926. The first wood to be gleaned from the mammoth trees was used for town and mill buildings. No mill like Long-Bell had ever before been constructed. It wasn't so much different from other Northwest mills, simply bigger, more mechanized, and better planned to produce lumber in vast quantities. It had 30 mill buildings that averaged 700 ft. in length, with some well over 1,000 ft.

In full production, Long-Bell was milling 2 million board feet of lumber a day, making it, briefly, the largest lumber producer in the nation. But in 1927, a decline in construction activity was making it more difficult for Long to sell his lumber. Capital assets had to be sold to keep the company alive. To make matters much worse, the market crash of 1929 brought the economy to a halt. Somehow, Long-Bell limped along until the war effort required increased production and the postwar housing boom further

To maximize production, the Long-Bell mill was huge, with 72 acres of building under roof. Many individual sawmills operated simultaneously, and for a time it had the greatest output of any mill in the world.
(PHOTO COURTESY LONGVIEW PUBLIC LIBRARY, LONGVIEW ROOM COLLECTION)

As Long-Bell is dismantled, the immense size of the individual buildings is revealed. The mill's sad story became a boon to many timberframe homeowners.
(PHOTO BY TEDD BENSON)

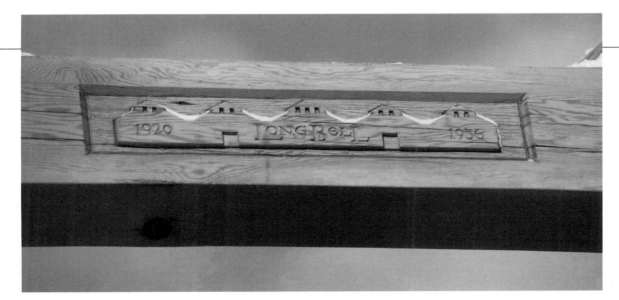

In homage to the Long-Bell mill, a relief of some of its buildings was carved into one of the timbers for a central Colorado home.

(PHOTO BY BILL HOLTZ)

revived the mill for a few years. But it was too little, too late. In 1956, the mills fell silent. New sawmill technology had made the whole Long-Bell facility and its equipment obsolete.

The Long-Bell mill buildings had been entirely constructed with large, old-growth timbers. In the years when they were built, clear, straight-grained fir flowed like manna from the ancient forests. When it was determined that the buildings would be dismantled, word quickly spread among timberframers, who knew that wood of that size and quality might never be seen again. But when the bids for the salvage rights began climbing, the timberframers began to wonder who else could want dirty, old timbers more than they would. (Bill Gates, for one, who wanted Long-Bell timbers for his home compound in Seattle.) It was estimated that more than 7 million board feet of timbers would be salvaged from the many buildings scheduled for dismantling, so any serious bidder would need deep pockets. It wasn't long before the prices escalated beyond the meager means of the average timberframer.

Still, Bill Gates couldn't use it all. So, over the next few years about 5 million board feet became available to timberframers around the country. It should therefore not be surprising that this magnifi-

cent wood made its way into quite a few of the homes featured in this book.

INTO THE FUTURE

I hope that someday in the far distant future (say around the turn of the 26th century) people will tell stories about some of the homes in this book. They would admire their durability and beauty (enhanced with age), and there would be much to say about their history. It is my dream that the houses would have survived both because they are inherently durable and because the occupants thought them worthy of maintenance and preservation. It is also my dream that at that future time they won't be historical relics but rather would have adapted to the needs of the inhabitants and the technology and style of the time.

Some of the buildings would perhaps no longer be homes, and that would be fine. For those that don't survive intact, it is realistic to think that their frames will be dismantled and re-erected or that the individual timbers will be used again. I don't believe we'll have to wait long before it is well understood that timbers such as you see in this book are precious. And when they move on to new buildings, they will come with stories, including the one from Long-Bell.

This central Montana timberframe was built entirely with timbers from the Long-Bell facility. There's every reason to believe that the building will last for hundreds of years, but if it must come down, its timbers can be used again. (PHOTO BY TEDD BENSON)

In

Architecture is the handwriting of man.... When you enter his domain you know his dreams.
—Bernard Maybeck, architect

the Country

Whether people are fully conscious of this or not, they…derive countenance and sustenance from the "atmosphere" of the things they live in or with.
—Frank Lloyd Wright

Prairie Prospect

"The home you design for us will be our dream home, the one in which we raise our children, celebrate holidays, and grow old." So said the owners in a questionnaire submitted early in the design process. The designers took the message to have a wider meaning: That home design is not really about physical matter—the concrete, bricks, stone, and wood—but about the people who will inhabit the home, how it functions for them, and how it might enrich their lives. Designing homes to reach this higher goal requires humility and listening skills.

The building sits on a windswept grassy slope with beautiful views in three directions. The owners felt that a horizontal, multilevel, cantilever-roofed Prairie-style home would fit nicely into the surroundings.

A confluence of connections is both an engineering event and a sculpture. Diagonal struts deliver building loads to this interior post on each of its four faces, while the laminated arch is connected with a complex joint at the post corner. A cherry spline provides additional joint strength.

left Celebrating the horizon views, grand space, and light, this room reflects the "big sky" landscape themes of central Nebraska. If the wall color seems bold, it is but a pale imitation of the stunning sunsets that inspired its hue.

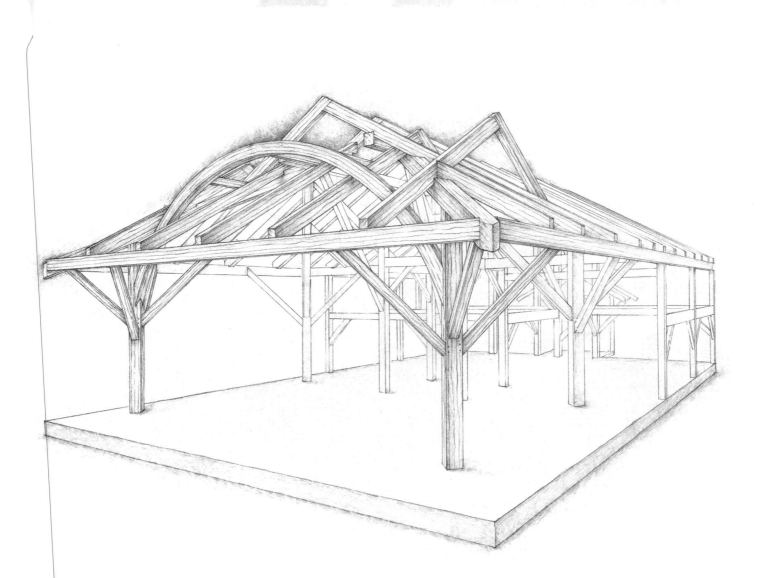

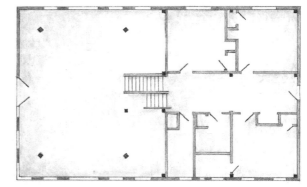

size
3,200 sq. ft.

completed
1997

location
Central Nebraska

The owners wanted a home that was a celebration of the timberframe space. "One of the many reasons we like timberframed homes is the expansive arched ceilings where you can admire the wood and joinery." The frame mixes salvaged Douglas fir from a western mill, salvaged southern yellow pine from an eastern bridge, and new eastern white pine. A laminated pine beam frames the eyebrow dormer. In the great room, all exterior wall loads are directed toward interior posts through diagonal struts.

In the kitchen, a commercial stove, laboratory countertops, brushed stainless-steel hardware, and salvaged industrial lights were chosen for utility and durability, not for "show"—utility and durability *are* the show in this house.

below Industrial details give the house a feeling of spare functionality. Stainless-steel cables, steel grating, and painted steel combined with cherry form the stair. Red oak Mission-style cabinets define and separate the kitchen but also, because they are built to furniture standards, are in keeping with the rest of the great-room spaces.

Directly inside the front entry, the first glimpse of the house gives evidence of the grand spaces and the interplay of steel and wood.

below A third-floor loft is actually a "monitor," which rises above the timberframed roof. The loft serves several purposes. In the heat of summer, it ventilates the building, aiding draft and exhausting heat. Year round, it provides extra sleeping space or a quiet place to read.

As a way of expressing to the designers their own passion for the Prairie landscape, the owners quoted Willa Cather, from *O Pioneers!* "For the first time…a human face was set toward [the land] with love and yearning. It seemed beautiful to her, rich and strong and glorious. Her eyes drank in the breadth of it, until her tears blinded her." The house had to rise from the land and connect the owners to it.

One of the most prominent features of the Nebraska landscape is the wide-open sky with views from one horizon to the next. The owners wanted to incorporate as much of this sky as possible into their home. A low band of windows, including corner windows, opens the house to the horizons, while the higher windows reveal the changing sky and allow light to penetrate deep into the space.

Ah! There is nothing like staying at home for real comfort.
—Jane Austen

Home Spirit

It isn't always possible to capture the true essence of a home with photography. For the owners of this house, the real "spirit of the house" has to do with the many things that have happened there. Their children grew up in the house, which has been the setting for countless gatherings, celebrations, and all the joys and sorrows that make up family life. "The timberframe spaces are 'people friendly' and wonderfully comforting," said one of the owners, as if speaking of another member of the family. Many of a home's most important attributes accrue over time through the lives of its inhabitants.

When you spend your days working in the nation's capital, the ideal home is a refuge of authenticity and integrity. Hidden in a deep, old forest of beech and oak, this home, like its occupants, exudes honest values.

"There isn't a warmer house in northern Virginia," said one of the owners, referring to the quality of light. She attributes the cast of light to the tone and texture of the impeccable Douglas fir in the frame.

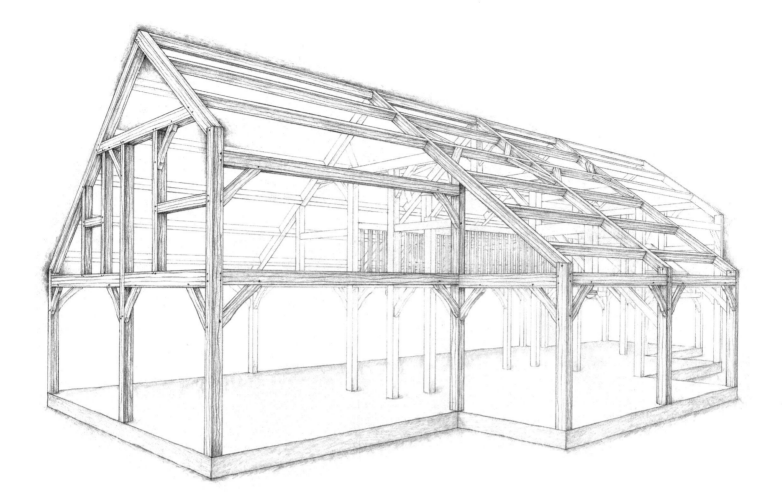

size
2,500 sq. ft.

completed
1987

location
Northeast Virginia

Arching over the bridge and the stairway in the great room is a hammerbeam truss. An ingenious structural device used to span large spaces, it transfers roof loads through post and beam brackets to the outer walls. The hammer-beam concept was developed during the Middle Ages by timberframers who were, by all evidence, the best of all time.

left The owners spend most of their time in this part of the house. The dining and kitchen areas are open to each other in a traditional country-kitchen arrangement. Because most families tend to congregate where food is prepared and eaten, dining is often the only time when the whole family is together in the course of a day. The open kitchen is the hearth of our times and should be designed to be special, spacious, and comfortable.

below A peaceful, light-filled solarium off the front entry is one of those special places that beckons use and is easily changed to suit. It is variously the family game center, a second dining area, a tearoom, and a private reading nook.

The bridge is real. It passes under the central hammer-beam truss and spans between second-floor bedrooms, which are separated by the two timber bays of the great room. Oversize handrails are structural upper chords, tied to the lower chords through several balusters.

We have from the first planned houses that are based on the big fundamental principles of honesty, simplicity, and usefulness.
—Gustav Stickley

Craftsman's Way

Around the turn of the century, the Arts and Crafts movement—with its emphasis on hand craftsmanship and the simple display of natural materials—began to have a strong influence on American architecture. Its most recognized masters were the Greene brothers and Bernard Maybeck of California, but it was primarily popularized by Gustav Stickley. The timberframe re-

vival, which began in the 1970s, springs from the same philosophical roots. In this Washington state home, the two strands merge in a wonderful display of their respective attributes.

A rail detail on the stair landing uses a joint common in Mission furniture (note the chair arms, facing page), which also arose from the Arts and Craft movement. Exposing joint elements and celebrating the beauty of wood is also a central theme of timberframing.

Deep overhangs and carved beam and rafter ends are typical Arts and Crafts details. The recessed window adds dimension to the lines of the otherwise basic building shape and gives emphasis to one of its simple, delightful features.

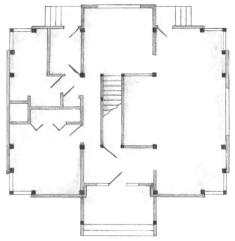

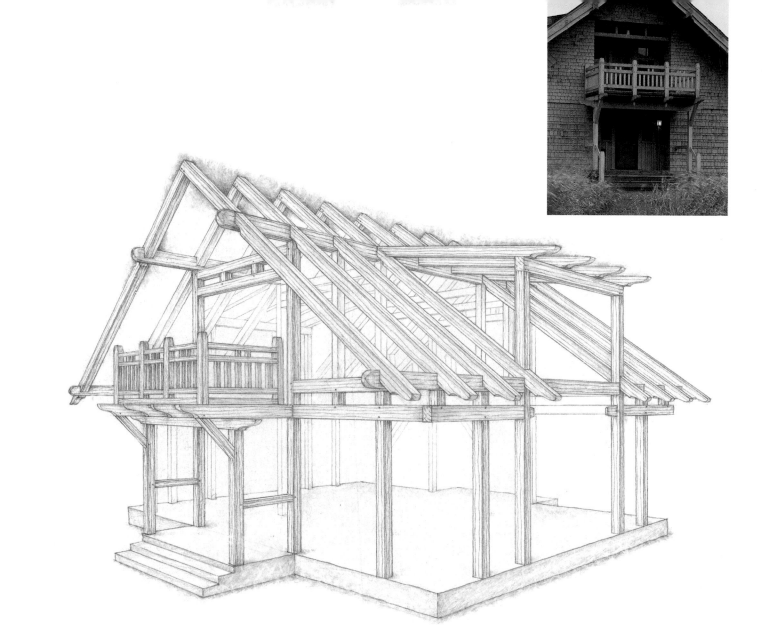

size
1,600 sq. ft.

completed
1994

location
Western Washington

Originating in Europe, the Arts and Crafts architectural style reveals the influence of the Swiss chalet, with its balconies and exposed timberframing in extended gable overhangs. Built with timber salvaged from the Long-Bell mill (see pp. 10-14), the frame has a sense of heritage in accord with the owner's collection of Mission furniture and handmade Arts and Crafts objects. Parallel beams were used on the exterior walls, substituting for typical diagonal bracing.

"We try to plan and build houses which will simplify the work of home life and add to its wholesome joy and comfort....We have paid particular attention to the convenient arrangement of the kitchen." (Gustav Stickley)

below As evidenced by this home's small size but expressive character, trading quantity of space for the best qualities of design, craftsmanship, and materials is a basic tenet of the Craftsman style.

left In the words of Gustav Stickley, "We like to have pleasant nooks and corners which give a comfortable sense of semi-privacy and yet are not in any way shut off from the larger life of the room." The doubled beams—or plates—above the windows provide the strength that allows each of the corners to be opened to a wrap-around window.

*Have nothing in your home that
you do not know to be useful or believe to be beautiful.*
—William Morris

England West

There was never any doubt about the architectural style. Although the house is located near Denver, it was to have a decidedly English country influence. One of the owners had spent some time in England and had become enthusiastic about the casual formality of this style. Also,

English immigrants heavily affected Colorado's Front Range architectural heritage, especially in the 40 years bridging the turn of the 20th century. So, the design was a fit both of taste and context. The interior takes on the feeling of a manor house and recalls the elaborate open halls that were common in the Middle Ages.

A poorly built, run-down bungalow was torn down to make room for the new house. Because the site contained mature landscaping, pains were taken during construction to preserve the setting. The covered entry is weather protection for visitors and for the cherry-wood entrance door.

Tall patio doors surround the dining room, giving it the feeling of a porch and connecting it to the terrace and the parklike landscaped acreage. The timbers are salvaged Douglas fir, recovered from the Long-Bell mill (see pp. 10-14). When the owners toured the timber yard to look at the various options, the mention of Long-Bell sparked a distant memory in one of the owners: Her grandfather had been the treasurer of the Long-Bell mills. The choice was made.

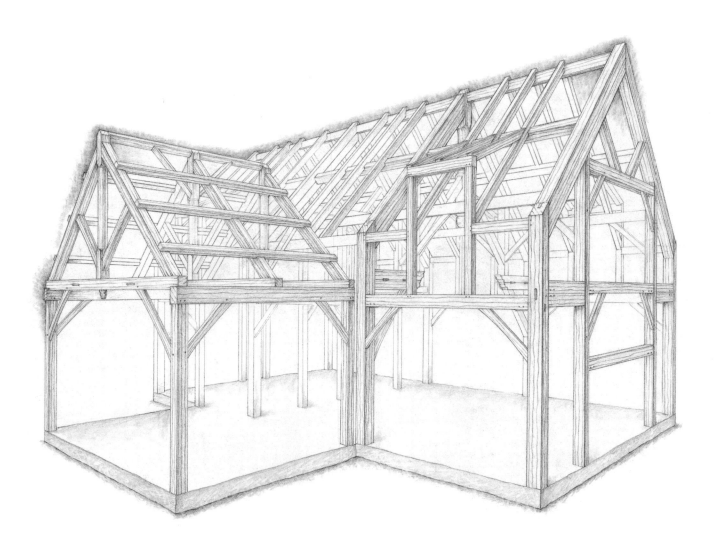

size
5,000 sq. ft.

completed
1993

location
Central Colorado

The house is specifically zoned. Private bedrooms and utility spaces are standard stud-frame, while the public spaces are timberframed. In this type of hybrid, it is important to keep the ties between the two framing types nonstructural, due to different patterns of settling. The principal-purlin and common rafter roof-framing configuration is common in traditional English-style construction. The frame is elaborated with chamfering, carved timber ends, and the use of cherry for joint details.

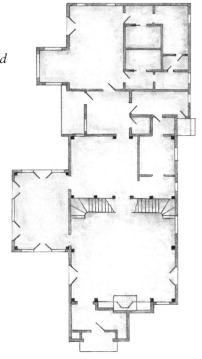

left The open-timber-roofed space is made up of three "bays," which are spaces between the structural cross sections, or "bents." Two bays form the vaulted great-room space, while the third bay is floored over to create a loft. The loft has two study nooks and serves as the home's library. It also provides passage to the second-floor bedrooms.

Although there is little headroom at the low side of the roof slope, no space is wasted. With a shed dormer to provide light, ventilation, and a spatial lift, the result is an intimate, inviting space, efficiently used.

A king post terminates many of the structural members in the center of the great room. The post features inset cherry panels and a carved pendant. Spaces on the top side of the central roof purlin and the ridge beam are used for indirect lighting.

Master woodworking skills were needed for the curved cornice-like treatment of this range hood. Diamond-shaped pegs are end-grain cherry. And what's the least expensive way to get a copper detail on the cabinet pulls? Polished pennies.

left For color and grain consistency, salvaged fir used for the kitchen-cabinet panels came from the same stock of wood as the timberframe. The cabinet drawer and door frames are cherry. Granite and copper complete the palette of materials. The kitchen is chock-full of custom design details for serious gourmet cooking.

The spiral stair is the main access to the upstairs bedrooms and to the recreation room on the ground floor. Looking from the master bedroom into the kitchen, it's evident that the private spaces are not timberframed.

below Primary exterior materials—limestone, brick, stucco, and slate—were chosen for low maintenance and longevity. The half-timber accents were gleaned from piles of wood salvaged from the original timber surfaces. Roofing is Vermont slate. The house is roughly halved, with the public timberframe spaces on the right and private bedrooms and bathrooms in the stud-framed part of the building on the left.

Concord Barn

For several weeks in 1989, twenty million people watched a real drama unfold on PBS's *This Old House.* As the series opened, plans developed to renovate a Concord, Massachusetts, barn into a new home.

However, it was discovered that the apparently sound timbers had rotted out due to a leaking roof early in the barn's history. It was a major setback: The frame had to be razed and replaced. The Timber Framers Guild of North America was quickly enlisted to build a new timberframe, demonstrate the trade skills to the viewing audience, and still keep the show on schedule. It was a tall order but good TV.

The original barn was built in 1845—not so long ago by timberframe standards—but the roof was allowed to leak for many years, which rotted the timbers and led to its razing.

Engineer Ben Brungraber sifted through the rubble of the razed barn to find any remaining structurally sound timbers. He found only a few diagonal braces, which became a vital link to the barn's history and so were used in the main living area.

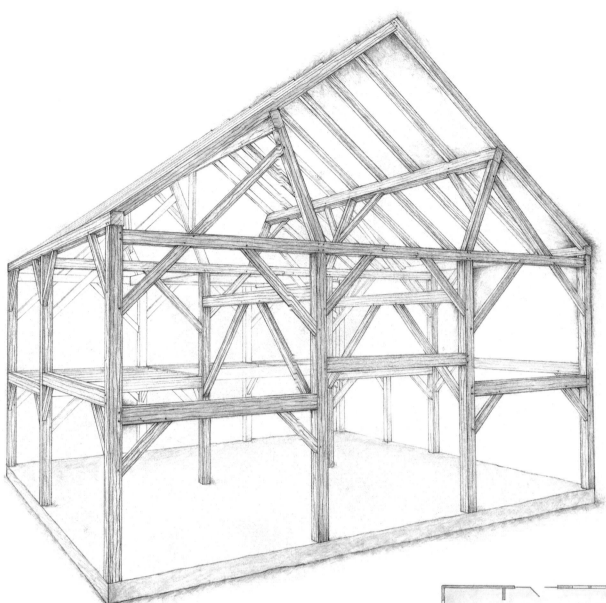

size
3,000 sq. ft.

completed
1989

location
Eastern Massachusetts

The shape of the new barn and the arrangement of timbers closely followed the original. Canted purlins with common rafters are typical of Early American barn framing. The entire frame was built by a class of 35 students, overseen by 6 professionals and aided by 30 volunteers. Making such a complex frame so quickly was an enormous feat.

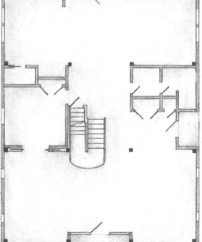

below Except for the plates on which the rafters sit and a few salvaged knee braces, the timberframe is built with eastern white pine. Steel stair railings are reminiscent of cow stalls and the building's agricultural roots.

Due to time and money constraints, only two timberframe bays were rebuilt. The third, containing kitchen and bedrooms, was built using structural insulated panels. A turned structural column also serves as a newel-post termination for the stair.

right Rustic sliding doors help maintain the barn's basic aesthetics, closing off a small, intimate study when privacy is desired. A barn is a barn, and less interior decorating is better. A hot water radiant-heating system is encased in lightweight concrete beneath the handmade clay-tile flooring.

The space within a building is the reality of that building.
—Frank Lloyd Wright

Vaulted Dwelling

This deceptively modest house was designed with minimal complexity, ornamentation, or architectural pretense. Its grand presentation was intended to be the interior, not the exterior. With their children grown, the owners wanted a single-floor living arrangement for themselves and ample room for visiting family and friends. The design takes advantage of the sloping site and places the secondary living areas on the ground floor. This decision

saved money and allowed the owners to make the living level more dramatic, with open timber roofs throughout.

What's dramatic here is not the building, but the woodland setting. Located in the Greater Boston area, the natural beauty and privacy of the site are almost startling. The house is in thrall to its environment.

In timberframe design, the principal columns and beams of the frame naturally delineate and define the rooms. Here, the kitchen is separated from the dining area not by a wall but by structural members. Less is more. East-oriented roof windows allow the morning sun into the kitchen area. A network of floor joists forms a trellised ceiling, which creates a sense of lower enclosure while still allowing the light to spill through from above.

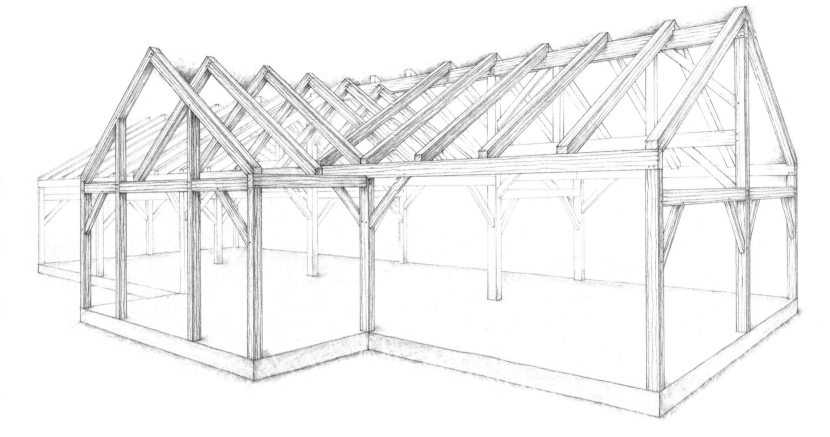

size
3,500 sq. ft.

completed
1994

location
Eastern Massachusetts

Resembling a Native American long house, the exterior simplicity of this building belies the intention and majesty of its interior. Salvage Douglas fir from a western mill building was used for the frame. Three 65-ft. timbers used as outside plates and ridge beam define the building's longitudinal orientation, and woven rafters are a feature at the cross-gable.

below Where gables cross, rafters interweave, and the sense of tension between the opposing gables is enhanced. The masonry chimney falls outside the structure of the living room, which helps maintain the unbroken space.

From the kitchen, the top of the living room "roof" is visible, which suggests an additional building form within the larger building and further defines the living area. The last pair of rafters are actually braces projecting from the central wall posts to the ridge.

Wood, stone, and tile are basic building materials and almost always work well together. Cherry is used here for the cabinets. Its reddish tones and natural elegance mate well with the other materials, especially the fir, which is complementary but has a rustic appearance.

A subtle alcove gives a little more room for the bed, while also creating a lighting soffit and breaking up a rather tall wall. The blackened notch in the post is a remnant of the timber's former life in the Long-Bell mill building.

A striking building stands before us
as an individual every bit as soulful as we are.
—Thomas Moore, author of *Care of the Soul*

Time Crafted

The 18th-century saltbox home needed no amendment. Its proportions were right, and its historical authenticity deserved preservation. Still, the owners required additional space if the property was to function well for their family. The wise solution was to build a complementary

new building rather than compromise the old one. What grew out of this decision is a traditional carriage-style barn that blends new and old. Amenities and functionality are modern, but the building features an old tower clock and 200-year-old reclaimed barn timbers.

Encircled with windows, the cupola is a kaleidoscope in wood: a play of symmetry, convergence, and light. And though its space is inaccessible for use, the barn and the living areas within seem bound to its axis.

If protected from decay, there's no reason the timbers should not last indefinitely. Most of the timbers in this frame are at least 200 years old and being put to use here for the second time. Remarkably, some of the timbers are clearly in their third structural use, having been salvaged from a previous building before being used for the barn that was dismantled to make this building. Old barn boards were used for the ceiling.

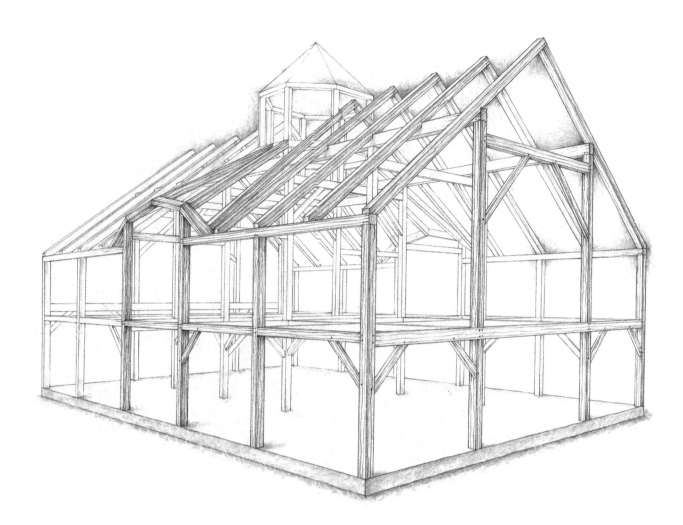

size
3,500 sq. ft.

completed
1997

location
Eastern Massachusetts

Salvaged timbers come from dilapidated barns with leaking roofs, failed foundations, or worse. Therefore, every timber has to be inspected for rot or structural defects. In addition, most barns were under-built by today's standards, making it difficult to find timbers of adequate size for some of the modern loads they must carry. The timbers for this frame were winnowed from the salvage piles of four barns.

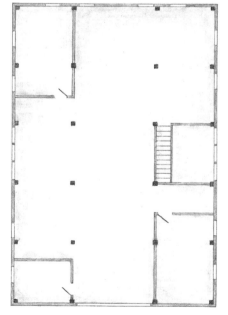

left Spline joinery and short sections of barn timbers were used to create the eyebrow lift to the roofline. Changing roof angles made the rafter-joint geometry complex. As is the case here, posts and beams, not walls, often define timberframe spaces.

right The cupola's spin of light and towering volume has a powerful effect on everything below.

below The barn—a short distance from the family's 18th-century home—is simply a detached addition. The lower level holds a three-car garage and a study, while the upper level has two guest bedrooms and a place for social gatherings and recreation. A natural oak log supports the post at the enclosed entry.

An 1870s tower clock is both whimsical and functional: The turning gears and oscillating pendulum provide fascination and inspire appreciation, while the 8-ft. translucent clock face is a primary source of daylight. Whitewashed boards reflect the natural light to brighten the space despite the predominance of darkly aged salvaged barn wood used for the roof boards and timbers.

With a turn of the eave and an oversize octagonal cupola topping the ridge, an otherwise simple structure of barn proportions appears much more complex, elegant, and sophisticated. But here function trumps ornamentation: These exterior features provide critical space and light to the interior.

The owners wanted two guest bedrooms, but closing them in was a problem. If their partitions extended to the roof, the great space of the barn's second floor would have been disrupted. The solution was to put the rooms at opposite corners for privacy and retain the open space.

left A carved limestone fireplace, painted paneling, and leather furniture transform this corner of the barn into a baronial lounge. The deep, charccal blue paint is particularly inspired, bringing more effect than color and recalling the feeling of pub more than parlor.

A board meeting in the barn? Why not. The unusual, heavily chamfered hewn post in the foreground was discovered in the basement of a gristmill in East Berne, New York. Each timber brings its own unique history to this new building.

How the eye loves a genuine thing;
how it delights in the nude beauty of the wood!
—John Burroughs, naturalist

Horse Haven

In beautiful rolling hills north of Baltimore, horses reign. The land is given over to grazing pastures, riding rings, prim barns, and orderly white fences. It's a landscape of formal utility, a place that recalls its productive agricultural past and is still habit-bent to feed with its fertile soil. When the owners of this home and horse farm decided to

build on a knoll overlooking their acreage, they knew they wanted to honor the area's traditional architecture by complement rather than reproduction. In the end, the design became a barn home overlooking pastureland.

A grand, open-timber-roofed great room looks in three directions. It has enchanting views, near, far, and inward. The big space is a solitary retreat or an accommodation for large gatherings.

Elegant timberframe engineering is revealed from this loft. Structural solutions in timberframe home building are also meant to be pleasing to the eye, even emotionally gratifying. Because most timberframe buildings are insulated with foam-core panels, the usual assumptions about heat layers in tall spaces such as this do not apply. In fact, the insulating method yields such a high R-value and low air-exchange rate that large spaces help keep the air fresh.

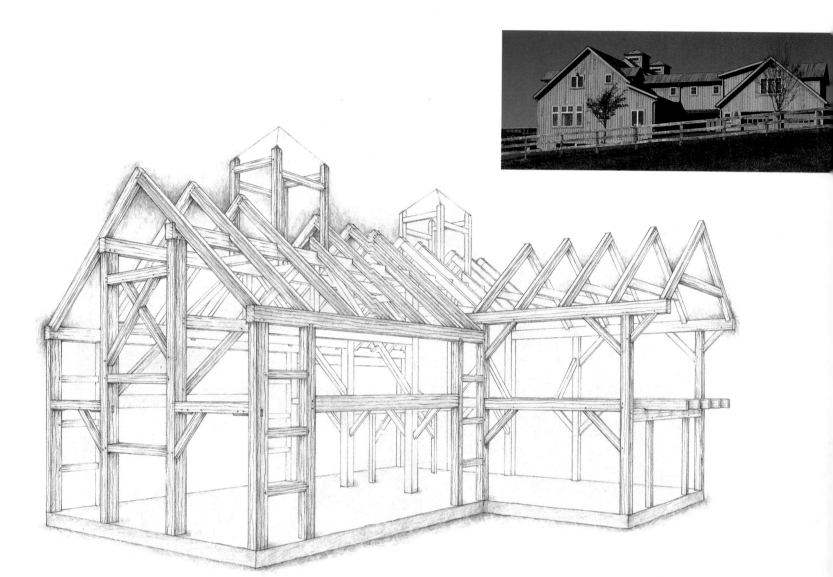

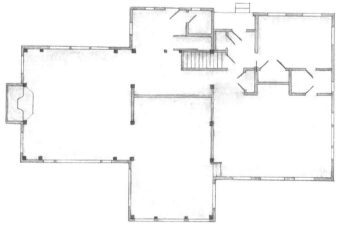

size
3,700 sq. ft.

completed
1994

location
Northeast Maryland

Long timbers and large braces create an uninterrupted space for the great room. Four parallel timber walls emphasize the aisle's organization and provide bearing for the cupola frames. Timberframing gives distinction to the most public living areas and to the master bedroom. The rest of the home's spaces are framed conventionally.

left Country furniture, an old woodworking bench, and salvaged fir timbers make the dining room casual and comfortable. This is the center of domestic activities and the place where the family is most likely to linger in conversation. With so many distractions to pull children and adults into isolation—television, stereo, computer games, telephone—the dining room has replaced the hearth as the place where this family is most likely to gather each day.

Located over the kitchen/dining area in the cross-gabled ell, the master-bedroom suite looks out over the pastoral landscape. Surrounded by light and views, the room is further enhanced by the open timbered ceiling, while the ceiling-height collar ties give a defining break to the volume.

Located at the crossroads of the family room, dining room, and great room, a wormy chestnut island, built with reclaimed barn wood, forms the home's hub. The post-and-beam arrangement distinguishes the spaces and keeps the plan open.

below An architectural synthesis gives the home and barn a strong relationship. Plain lines, vertical siding, metal roofing, and a pair of cupolas help to lean the home's design toward an agricultural motif.

A timberframe

creates (and is created by)

a more settled landscape

than a balloon frame.

—Michael Pollan,
A Place of My Own

On the Water

There is an undiscovered beauty, a divine excellence, just beyond us.
Let us stand on tiptoe, forgetting the nearer things, and grasp what we may.
—Bernard Maybeck, architect

Timber Bonded

Underlying the design of this pair of buildings—a house and a library—was a lofty and elusive idea the owners wanted to see reflected in their home, an idea they described to the designers as "The Circle and The Bond." The circle symbolizes family, community, seasons, and

the owners' day-to-day lives in their inner-island sanctum. This ideal is manifest in the house's circular traffic pattern. Commitment and responsibility are "the bond," represented by the timberframe, with its structural integrity, strength, and legendary endurance.

Appearing to float in the glade, the library was positioned so that one would feel free of moorings, in a place where thought and imagination might sail away.

top and left "Simplicity and integrity are the hardest things to achieve," according to the owners, who acknowledged that their intangible desires were the most elusive. Stripped of artifice and ornament, the home's design is all about scale, symmetry, and proportion.

When you have a home on a quiet and beautiful spot on an island, life is not spent indoors: The wraparound porch gets a lot of use.

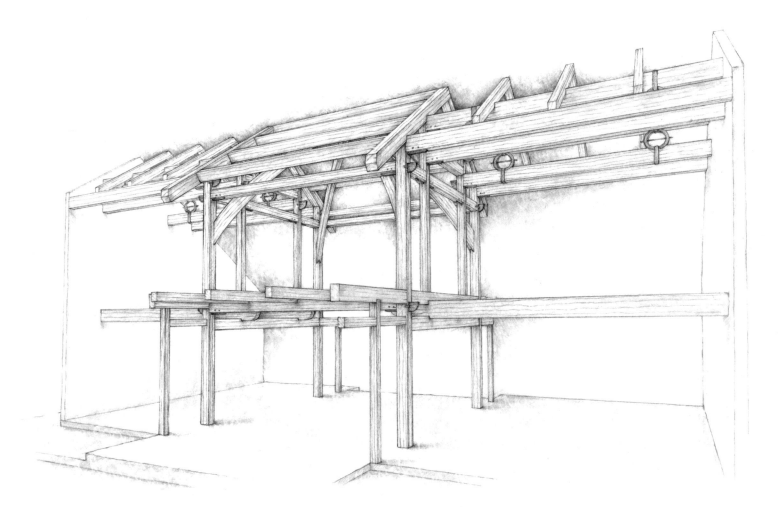

size
3,500 sq. ft.

completed
1993

location
Nantucket Island,
Massachusetts

A typical stud frame and timber-frame coexist in the house. The "livable sculpture" (the owner's reference to the timberframe) is entirely inside the exterior walls. With the exception of a couple of notable features, the timber structure is spare and straight-forward. In the central bay, laminated curved timbers create a vaulted feeling under the ridge, while also serving as bracing for the whole structure. In the outer bays, rafters bear on parallel beams that are tied together by iron rings to make the long span.

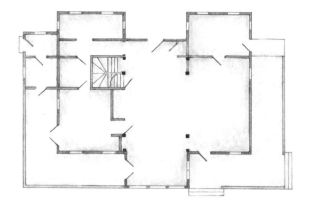

"Ornament is the adoration of the joint," declared architect Louis Kahn, suggesting that it is the connections and transitions between elements and materials that are the natural embellishments of a building. Cherry splines and wedges interplay with fir timbers and a blackened iron bracket to achieve both structure and decoration.

below Contemporary timberframe design and construction is a present-day Arts and Crafts movement, combining good design, traditional building materials, and skilled work. Here, a black slate proscenium celebrates the hearth, and an opening atrium lifts the space beyond its confines.

The master bedroom is open to the bathing area of the bathroom, which enlarges the space while expressing the owners' sense of intimacy. Evidence of the timbers' former life in the Long-Bell mill can be seen in the plugged bolt holes and nail stains. The load-transfer mechanism between the beams is an iron ring with a rod through it, which symbolizes the project's philosophical theme—The Circle and The Bond.

Curved, laminated timbers converge over the atrium opening to the first floor. A walkway around the atrium opening provides circular access to the second-floor spaces. The rope? Well, things can be lowered or lifted. It's more useful than you might think.

below Restraint and simplicity were design and construction watchwords. The design team and building crew were often reminded that less is usually harder to achieve than more. It helped to keep the variety of wood species restricted. Salvaged fir was used for the timberframe; cherry for interior doors, trim, and exposed joint parts; ash for the floors and stairs. The timberframe rests on conventional exterior walls.

Seen from the far side of a bordering cranberry bog, the house rises up and looks outward, toward the horizon, while the library hunkers down, looking inward.

below For the frame timbers, it's a long way from the industrial setting of the Long-Bell mill to the sophisticated and scholarly ambience of this library.

Welcome to the "bog room," the gabled room that overlooks the cranberry bog. From this vantage point, you can see the distant ocean as well as the interior island, with its wildlife, vegetation, gnarled forest, and unique landscape.

Space, structure, texture, light—these are less the elements of a technology than the elements of an art.
—Joseph Hudnut, architect

Light Hall

In the decades following the Civil War, as industry blossomed along the East Coast and in the Midwest, great factories and mill complexes were constructed at a furious pace. Until the early part of the 20th century, when it was nearly harvested out (and eventually replaced by

steel beams), longleaf southern pine provided the framework for these vast buildings. This lakeside home utilizes the salvage from one of those 19th-century factories. It seems fitting that after 100 years of service the timbers have come to "retire" in a warm, well-lit space where they are cherished by the inhabitants.

Inspired by Japanese timberframe construction, a single natural-form timber, called a taiko beam, is featured in an otherwise rectilinear framework. The beam is intended to give tribute to the trees from which the timbers came.

The timberframe raising, usually accomplished in a single day, is always a dramatic event. At the end of the day, the sculptural form of a timberframe structure stands against the evening sky, almost always inspiring a celebration. During the course of that celebration, someone will inevitably stare wistfully at the frame and say, "It's a shame to cover it up. We should just enclose it in glass." These homeowners weren't kidding.

size
6,000 sq. ft.

completed
1995

location
South Carolina

In the medieval tradition, this home is essentially an open timberframe hall, flanked by secondary living spaces. In the entry foyer and adjacent kitchen, a hybrid structure with interior timber posts and ceiling joists connects to stud-framed exterior walls, thereby extending the timberframed look to all the public areas. The two timberframed structures intersect at the roof in valley timbers, where complex joinery is required.

Overlooking the great room, a balcony study enjoys a special perch. The study receives light from the high windows and has a view to the lake. The compound-angle roof connections, visible in the background, require strong timberframe skills.

below In the kitchen, only the ceiling is timbered, but it's enough to give continuity to the space, which overlooks the dining room and the "glass hall." Like the timbers, the pine flooring is also salvaged from an industrial building, this one with a tasty history—the Hershey chocolate factory.

left Although the dining area is open to the great room, a sense of intimacy is achieved by locating it under the balcony. As is common in timberframe design, spatial definitions tend to correspond to zones defined by post and beam placement.

Island Sentinel

A hand-painted sign down by the Nantucket ferry dock used to read: "Boat to America." Nantucket is far enough out in the ocean that it almost feels like foreign territory—a place with its own unique culture and its own way of doing things. In the old days, the island's wealth came from whaling. Seafaring men were pragmatic about design but demanding about construction quality. When the going got rough, they knew what mattered. Today, land values are the real wealth on Nantucket, yet the houses being built there clearly grow out of the whaling heritage. Drawing from that history, this house was built to ship standards, prepared to face the open ocean with integrity and respect.

The "barn" contains spaces for recreation and exercise, as well as a complete guest apartment. Another guestroom is in the pool house, at left. On Nantucket, choosing the exterior siding is easy: shingles are mandatory.

below Carved Douglas fir columns and curved beams define a central arcade through the barn guest quarters. Warmed by the many wooden surfaces, light from the cupola and dormers gives the space a luxurious glow.

One of the first things you discover when you build a nice home in a spectacular setting is that you have more friends than you thought. Guestrooms are needed everywhere. The pool-house guestroom features diamond-oriented Port Orford cedar frame members.

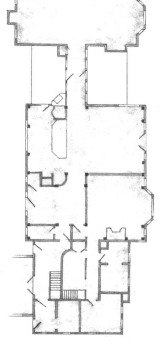

size
7,500 sq. ft.

completed
1990

location
**Nantucket Island,
Massachusetts**

The frame section shown above represents only the central structure of the main house. Each wing is a separate timberframe. In plan, the buildings are organized to create a courtyard area, which includes a swimming pool. Though the entire project could be achieved only by the affluent, the individual buildings provide instructive lessons in proportionate design and functional luxury on more modest scales.

above According to legend, the wives of Nantucket's seafaring men had rooftop decks built so they could look out to sea and watch for the ships to come home. The men didn't always return, and the roof decks came to be known as "widow's walks." Today, the roof deck is simply a place with a great view.

right The grand size of this home is reduced architecturally to cottage scale by connecting a series of small structures. Viewed from the dining area, a timber colonnade leads to the living room (seen at left, above), revealing the unity of the interior spaces despite the apparent exterior separation.

left A paneled, movable wall was built between the kitchen and the dining area. The idea was to allow the kitchen to be closed from the dining room on an occasional basis, dictated by the formality of the function and the mess in the kitchen. Here, the attractive closed panels have won out over the open kitchen.

below A cozy corner by the fireplace in the living room is inspired by the style common to timberframe buildings of the 17th and 18th centuries. Discreet chamfers with decorative stops soften the timber edges. The planed and oiled finish and the high ceilings are qualities more common to contemporary timberframed homes.

Framed with Port Orford cedar timbers, the study has the integrated, crafted feel of a ship captain's galley. One of the truly unique wood species in the world, Port Orford cedar is strong, light, and moisture resistant. It is also reputed to be one of the few woods from which one cannot get a splinter (which is why it has commonly been used for stadium seats).

right A shed dormer lifts a sloping roof enough to make a second-floor bedroom spacious and light-filled. Keeping the rooflines low gives the large home a more modest appearance.

Yellow wallpaper and fabrics heighten the bright outlook of this bedroom, while Port Orford timbers and roof boards lend a warm and elegant rusticity. In conventional framing, opening the space to the rafters would have little aesthetic benefit; in timberframing, roof space is always too compelling to hide.

*The stone and wood in construction bear the same relation to architecture
as the piano does to the music played upon it.*
—Bernard Maybeck, architect

World Apart

Imagine what it would be like to live on your own small island. You get there by boat, which makes living there a real commitment of time and effort. Your 15-acre island is too small to warrant its own vehicle, so walking is the primary mode of transportation, and provisions have to be carried to and from the boat dock. However, such inconveniences are also an advantage. Although the

home is not far from the bustle of southern Connecticut, your island (your world) is a world away. With that seclusion in mind, the owners of this island timberframe built a relaxing home for family and friends that is dedicated to the enjoyment of life at a quieter pace.

Attached firmly to the island rock and built stoutly with stone and timber, the house is resolutely prepared for the tough weather it will surely endure.

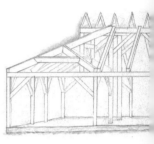

Parallel-chord
timber trusses are
used to span the
length of the great
room. The frame-
work adds textured
layers to the space
and thereby brings
the perceived ceil-
ing level down.
Spectacular stone-
work maintains the
quality and craft of
the timberframe
and is the focus of
the great room.
Porthole windows
continue the nauti-
cal theme.

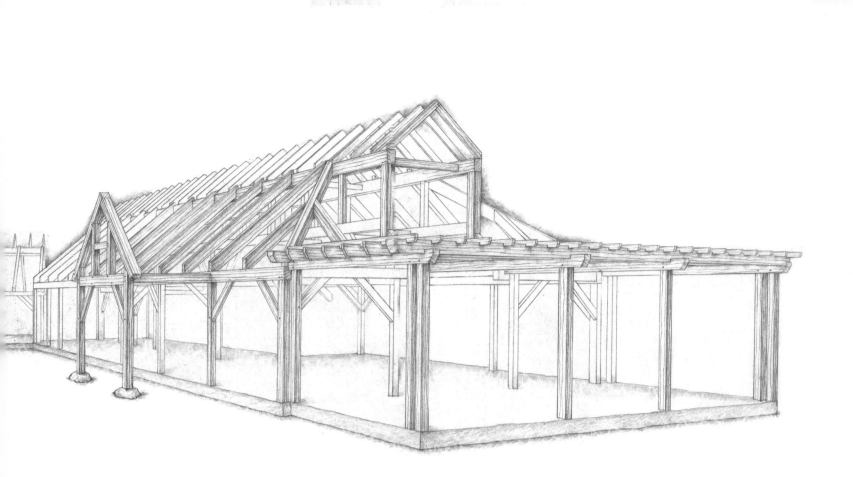

size
3,900 sq. ft.

completed
1996

location
Connecticut

The two upper mid-plates in the main timberframe are 70 ft. long (see p. 99 for a view of one of the continuous plates). They came from the Long-Bell mill, where they were lower chords of 72-ft. trusses. The Port Orford trellis covering makes a semiprotected outdoor space in the pergola and shades the south-facing glass of the great room. In plan, the house is configured to create a wind-buffered courtyard on the entry side.

Nestled into the natural terrain and lying low on the horizon, the home is designed to deflect the wind. You can't go wrong with natural building materials and basic building forms.

right Wood species traditional to boat building were used for exterior applications: Port Orford cedar for the timberframing of the entry and pergola, mahogany for the entrance and trim boards. A terrace of stone and the rubble-stone base wall ground the house to its rocky setting.

Right Cherry splines and wedges help to make rugged connections in the salvaged fir frame. A huge timber, which had long been waiting a proper use, found a home with owners who welcomed the bold and unusual. The carved date ensures that their wedding anniversary won't easily be forgotten.

Port Orford "staves" wrap the base of the stair and are contrasted by the cherry treads and railing. Salvaged fir balusters and newel post are from the same lot of wood as the timberframe. The glass-lined corridor connects the "dormitory" wing to the great room.

right Located at the crook of the building, the master bedroom has an unusual shape. But whatever might be different about the bedroom pales in comparison to what's different about the bed. Feeling the need for a touch of whimsy, the owners chose a bed that looks like something right out of a Disney movie.

left It's a child's dream space: a loft over the bedroom nearly as large as the bedroom itself. Painted the color of the evening sky, the loft is a perfect place for a pajama party or for a private getaway—an in-home tree fort.

...architecture as we know it is unimaginable without the tree.
—Michael Pollan, *A Place of My Own*

Tree House

Early in the design process, when the owners had only a basic notion of where their house would be built, a large white pine tree stood where the house would go. That's when they came up with the idea of building the house around the tree. The location of the house was later

changed and the tree didn't have to be cut down, but the designers and the owners held onto the idea of using a tree as a central column in the house frame. With some help, a 5-ft.-diameter red-cedar log was found moldering on the forest floor in Oregon and was "transplanted" on the lakeside New Hampshire site.

On the second level, a bridgelike connection ties the outer wings to the octagonal central hall. Diagonal struts to the roof structure are the tree's grafted branches.

right All the timberframe material came from the Long-Bell mill: Nothing else can substitute for the authentic character and patina of time. Three knee braces project to respective beams at one of the corners of the octagon.

It's entirely fitting that Stickley furniture would be used in a timberframe environment. Gustav Stickley was the leading popularizer of the early-20th-century Arts and Crafts movement. Its proponents advocated that the elements of craftsmanship should be made visible in furniture and building—also a central tenet of contemporary timberframe design.

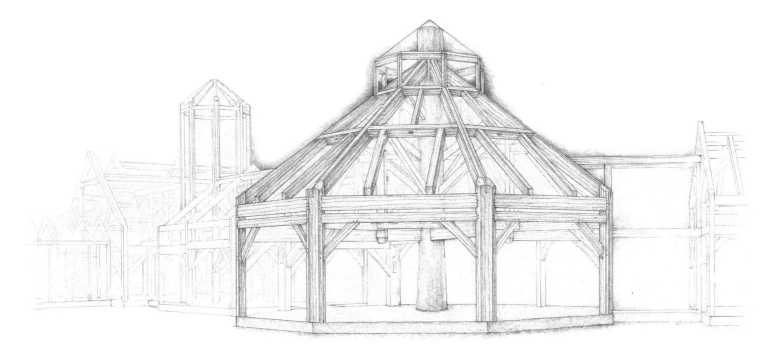

size
5,000 sq. ft.

completed
1993

location
Northern New Hampshire

The basic organization of this home is logical and simple, but it took a great deal of work to draw out the simplicity. An octagon core, which serves as the central public hall, is flanked by gabled wings, which house bedrooms and the kitchen. Only at the garage end does the home become more complicated. A stairway tower leads to the second-floor space, to the basement, and to a guest suite over the garage. It also leads to a great view.

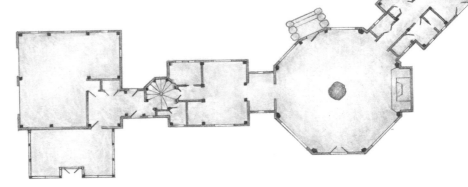

above The lakeside solarium is an elegant transitional space—the place to be on a chilly morning or to take refuge in during New Hampshire's spring bug season. Timberframing and glass is a natural marriage.

right Every effort was made to give the home a low profile to reduce its visibility from the lake. The siding color was chosen to blend with the surrounding tree bark and the roof color with the tree needles and leaves. A perimeter stone base grounds the house to the site. (PHOTO BY BRIAN SMELTZ)

left Fir framing, cherry treads, and Port Orford cedar planking are the wood medley for the stair tower. There's a great view from the top of the tower; the view of the workmanship inside isn't bad either.

below With naturally compatible colors, cherry cabinet frames and cherry flooring are combined with salvaged fir panels and timbers in a partnership of the refined and the rustic. A "ribbing" of arched floor joists accentuates the colonnade leading to the stair tower and the back entry. The carved detail at the post reduction is repeated in the beam and in the oak spline that connects them.

Though the home is large, the scale of individual spaces throughout is reduced to make them more personal and cozy. In timberframe design, there are typically no attics. The area under the roofline is simply too useful and beautiful to be relegated to storage.

right Throughout the home, a limited palette of wood species is used. Salvaged Douglas fir, cherry, and Port Orford cedar interplay in the bathroom but are used in a consistent manner. The granite slabs in the kitchen and bathrooms were cut from the same stone.

above Custom-made doors combine cherry frames with salvaged Douglas fir panels. Leaving the pegs proud of the door surface is a detail derived from the timberframe.

right On the balcony overlooking the great room, the wide dormers create delightful alcove sitting areas where the roofline is otherwise low. Since timberframes are generally enclosed by attaching materials to the outside timber surfaces, the finish work is nearly done when the building has been enclosed.

Three things are to be looked to in a building: that it stand
on the right spot; that it be securely founded; that it be successfully executed.
—Goethe

On Rocks

You cannot live by the ocean and not be affected by it. For those who know the ocean well, its majesty and mystery can inspire a lifetime love affair. The owners of this house grew up on this rocky coastal site, and the home's design had as much to do with connecting them to the ocean as it did with protecting them from its elements. They knew this "bony" coast, knew where to put the house and how to capture the best views in the morning and in the evening. They also knew that any structure built by the sea needs to be firmly anchored. So they pinned the foundation to bedrock and built a timberframe.

Winding under a collar beam and king post, the stairway is tightly integrated into the home's design.

Since the owners had spent much of their lives on the land before deciding to build, they had an intimate knowledge about where best to site the house and how to organize the plan to take full advantage of the sun and views.

right Integrated into the main body of the home, the all-season porch is located in one of the corner quadrants as defined by the timberframe. Redwood window and panel units, made from decommissioned wine tanks, fit snugly into the post-and-beam framework.

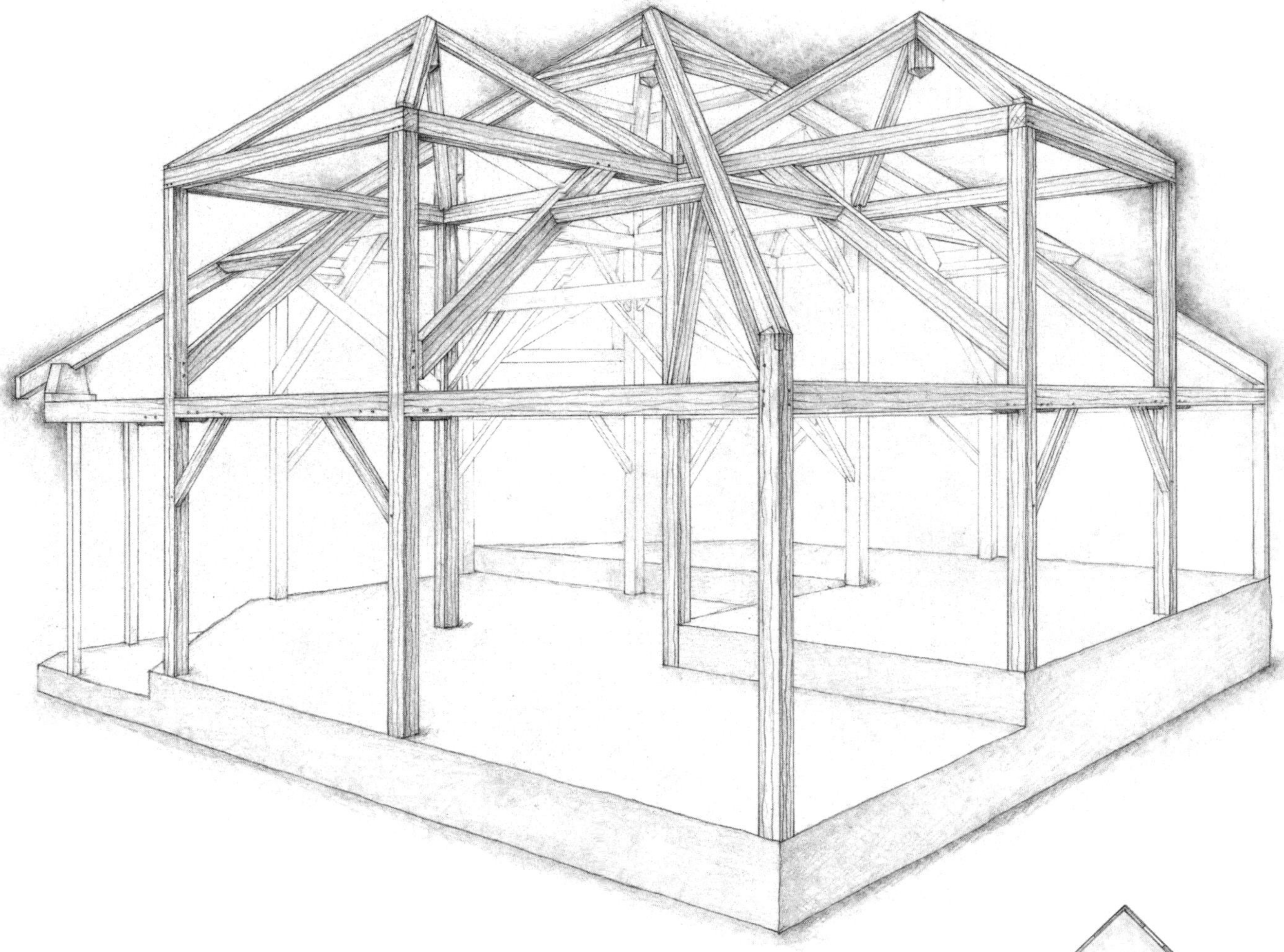

size
3,500 sq. ft.

completed
1993

location
Connecticut

The arrangement of the timberframe logically divides the footprint of the building into nine sections. By combining or separating the spaces as design needs suggested, there were numerous room-layout possibilities in this simple grid. From the interior, the hipped dormers create interesting timberframe pyramidal shapes, but the most important effect of the roof lift is that the dormers increase the second-floor living space.

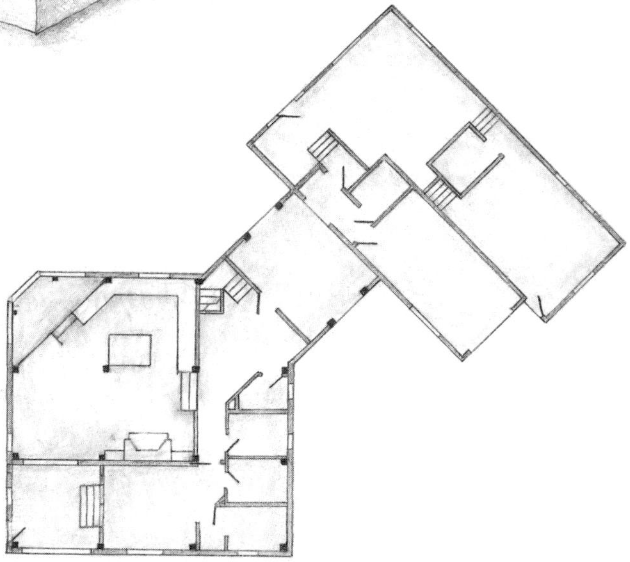

With 100-year-old salvaged fir timbers locked together with wooden splines and pegs, living in this timberframe space is like living in heirloom furniture. Here, one is surrounded by the elemental effect of wood and stone, in a lofty space where natural light is carried to the core. In such a place, one becomes convinced that the quality of life can be improved by the quality of the space one lives in.

below Loosely defined by the post-and-beam grid, an efficient kitchen space is opened to the other public living areas. Whitewashed ceiling boards maintain the wooden texture of the timber joists and brighten up the area.

right In an unusual orientation, one of the corners of the house is directed toward the owners' favorite view of the open ocean and a distant lighthouse. To allow a corner window placement, a large laminated timber directs building loads into cantilevered beams. The carving honors the Indian chief who "owned" the land before the English came.

*It is the nature of any organic building
to grow from its site, come out of the ground into light.*
—Frank L. Wright

Glass Bunker

In British Columbia, on the Gulf of Georgia island where this home is built, there is evidence of aboriginal settlement going back 3,000 years. The owners had lived in an old cottage on their land periodically for 20 years before deciding to build a permanent home. They took great interest in the discovery that there had been an ancient settlement on their land, but only when they discovered a 1,000-year-old skeleton not far from the house site did they come to appreciate that their location was sacred. Together with their architect, they determined that, in respect to the ancients who preceded them, they would design their new home to honor the land.

It's almost as if the house footprint was cut from the land with a giant knife so that a surface section could be lifted high enough to fit living spaces beneath. With its sod roof and transparent walls, the house is well camouflaged on its site.

A view through the central corridor shows how the home's spaces cascade downward from the entry, following the slope of the land. Acting like the home's spine, the corridor is the structural and spatial link to the two serpentine outer wings. Custom-laminated curved roof joists, topped by clear panels, light the passageway and extend the connection to the outdoors.

A wooden scarf joint is used to connect timbers to make up one of the two continuous beams that pass through the middle of the house. A central key and interlocking geometry keep the scarf joint tight.

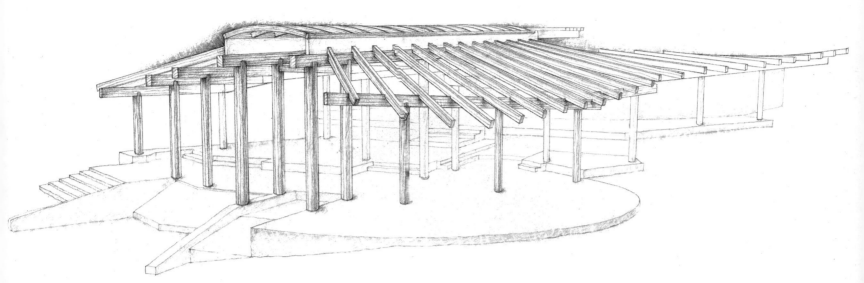

size
3,500 sq. ft.

completed
1994

location
**Gulf of Georgia,
British Columbia, Canada**

Made of salvaged Douglas fir, the timberframe structure posed special challenges because the shape and slope of the building meant that each rafter had to be a different length and pitch. The important design feat was to support the building loads inboard from the free-form glass panels, allowing the building's exterior walls to be liberated from typical configurations and so transparent as to be barely existent.

left The sandstone for the fireplace and chimney was quarried on the island and brought to the site by barge. A master mason custom-cut each stone and created a unique sculptural interplay of color and shape. Light-colored maple flooring helps brighten the interior.

above Looking through the kitchen space and the small study beyond, you can see how the interior plates, supported by peeled logs, allow the rafters to cantilever to the non-load-bearing glass curtain walls.

left To be inside a building designed in a natural form and built with natural materials and to be surrounded by walls of glass panels is essentially to be outside at the same time.

A heavy, wide entrance door is hinged away from the outside edge for better weight control and balance. The door's framework is part of the timberframe. Ingenious wooden hardware does all the work of its metal counterpart except allow the door to be locked. But then, why lock the door in a house of glass?

Privacy is not an issue in a secluded corner of an island, so why not be open to a great view of the gardens even while bathing or showering?

In an ancient time, the Saanich people built a longhouse not far from where this house sits. Part of the inspiration for the home came from that traditional form: The long, linear central corridor is the backbone of the design. A forest of peeled columns is an appropriate reflection of the home's natural setting.

...the dome of thought, the palace of the soul.
—Lord Byron

Bras d'Or Ark

At the northeastern end of Nova Scotia lies Cape Breton Island, a remote and beautiful place with a rich heritage and fabulous landscape. The island is nearly cut in half by a large saltwater lagoon, known as Bras d'Or Lake. Before deciding to build a permanent home overlooking the lake, the owner of this house had lived seasonally in a small cabin on the land for many years. Torn between

Cape Breton's majesty and the friends and culture of her former cosmopolitan home, she determined to a build a place that would support art and music and draw her many friends for visits.

As if steaming toward the horizon, this home is a "ship" with a mission. Part of the year, the house is given over to music and art education for young people, and occasional professional concerts are open to the community, turning the home into a music hall.

A view down through the dramatic central atrium reveals the home's three levels. Bedrooms are located on the ground level, along with the entry and utility rooms. The primary living spaces are on the second floor, and a loft with the highest outlook to the lake is on the third level. A handmade German kacheloven, or masonry stove, is capable of heating the entire open space.

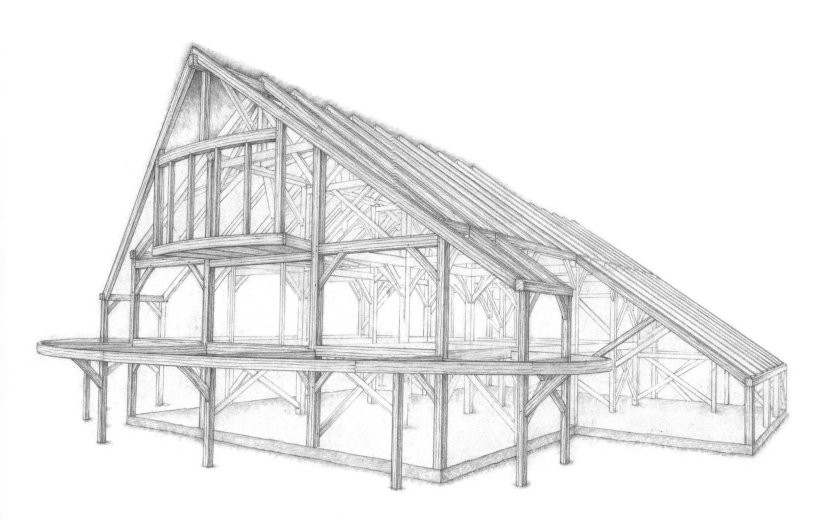

size
6,000 sq. ft.

completed
1990

location
**Cape Breton, Nova Scotia,
Canada**

Because the home is perched on a windy location high above the lake, the timber-frame was heavily braced in preparation for the worst of storms. Cross-bracing was used to bring about the necessary rigidity and was featured in the exposed structure. Double cross-braces in a timber truss span over the atrium (see the photo on the facing page). Laminated timbers give the curved shape to the upper cantilevered balcony and the outside deck.

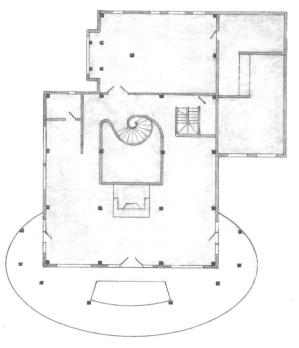

Douglas fir joists radiate outward to support the curved third-floor balcony in the living area. Wooden furniture was made from the same lot of wood as the timberframe to ensure compatibility of color and texture. The tiled corner fireplace is also a very efficient masonry heater and can radiate heat into the space for many hours after the fire is out.

above Redwood light fixtures and the fir timberframe have a harmonious relationship in their celebration of wood and craftsmanship. Exposed pegs in the beam secure a hidden hardwood spline.

right A pair of rounded columns defines an extended gable space that cantilevers over the ground level entrance. Typical of modern timberframe design, the timber arrangement and exposed joinery are meant to be both structural and sculptural. Light from the high gable window carries deep into the dining space beyond.

left The custom-made walnut dining table is crafted in a style popularized by George Nakashima, which celebrates the natural characteristics of the wood. Owners of timberframe homes find that the crafted quality of the frame tends to set a standard for finishes and furniture.

above Fabric and carpets bring rich colors and textures to this bedroom. Though most of the home's spaces are more restrained, the lavish decorating creates a place with a more luxurious and sensuous feeling. In this case, direct sunlight was not desired, so the bedroom is under the overhung exterior deck.

In the

A house is in many

ways a microcosm

of the landscape;

the landscape explains

the house.

—J. B. Jackson,
landscape theorist

Mountains

Reveal the nature of wood, plaster, brick or stone in your designs.
—Frank Lloyd Wright

High Plains Salvage

It was the perfect place for the owner's new ranch—a lush piece of land on the High Plains, sandwiched between mountain ranges and watered by runoff streams. The challenge was to build a house that wouldn't mar the beautiful landscape. Good ranch buildings are humble and pragmatic, worn by weather and use, rugged and persevering. The owner wanted his ranch to be that way, so it was designed to be simple and low-lying and built mostly with salvaged materials. Using peeled logs, old timbers, rocks from the land, and junk materials gathered from here and there, he built a sturdy, unique, and unaffected house.

If this building is a celebration of stone and wood, the two materials come together at the stairway in a joyous dance. Intermingling in the stair parts are juniper, lodgepole pine, willow, river birch, and heart pine. (PHOTO BY WILL BREWSTER/MERLE ADAMS)

Between 1901 and 1904, a remarkable 12-mile wooden railroad trestle, known as the Lucin Cut-Off, was constructed across the Great Salt Lake. The rafters and posts of this entry cover are salvaged pilings from that hard-worked trestle. The long immersion in salt water preserved the wood, some of which was cut into thin slabs and used to pave the entranceway—where the salt-impregnated slabs actually melt snow.

Were it not for the funky old building materials, the architecture might evoke a more contemporary intention. As it is, with so many construction treasures rescued from the maw of a landfill, the ranch's derivation and age are nicely unsettled.

size
4,800 sq. ft.

completed
1997

location
Central Montana

Pretense is not in the vocabulary of ranchers. Function and resource efficiency are more to the point. The frame is constructed with materials "harvested from the industrial forest" and gleaned from loggers' rejects. The structure is a testament to the sustainability of timberframing: The material for framing can come from old buildings and young trees and can live numerous useful lives.

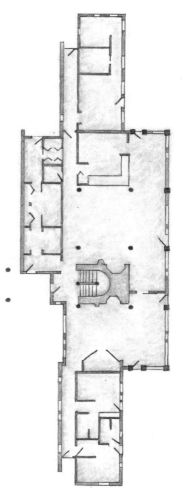

In the soft light of the late-afternoon sun, the home's low profile and natural materials seem very appropriate for the site.

(PHOTO BY WILL BREWSTER/MERLE ADAMS)

left Because the pieces of this timberframe are so natural, crooked, and unique, there had to be trust between the owner, architect, and builder. Many critical decisions were made not on paper, but in the timberframe shop or up in the air, where the pieces were joined.

right Salvaged: The rusted vent hood comes direct from a salvage yard; the door and cabinets are from beer and wine tanks; window frames and other beams are fir from old mill buildings; and the rafters are pilings from the Great Salt Lake railroad trestle.

It's all backwards on the garage. Siding is on the inside, structure on the outside; skeleton and skin are reversed, as they would be on an industrial building used to store bulk material. Salt Lake trestle pilings, mill timbers, and logs too-small-to-saw make up the frame.

left Vlasic pickles used to be made in tanks of cypress and redwood, but the modern tanks are stainless steel. All the siding here once knew pickles well.

Built in the late 1800s, the barn was an anchor for the new house. It defined the place and influenced the style. The barn's construction is a combination of stacked logs and conventional stud framing. Timberframing was not used much in the rapid westward expansion because of the skill and time required.

(PHOTO BY WILL BREWSTER/MERLE ADAMS)

*The eye craves lines of strength, evidence of weight
and stability…. Hence the lively pleasure we feel…in every architectural
device by which the real framework of the structure, inside or out,
is allowed to show, or made to serve as ornament.*
—John Burroughs, naturalist

Mountain Manor

Not since the Middle Ages have timberframe structures been so expressive. Now, as then, the organization of the timbers within the frame may have additional design intent and structural members may double as carved ornamentation. Compare this home's frame with that

of Little Hall (pp. 210-214) and with the elaborate frames in the town of Lavenham (pp. 215-217) and you'll see more similarities than differences, despite the 600-year age gap. The kind of space created in the modern timberframe, with its soaring volumes and the interplay of parts, is an old idea. The new ideas are light and comfort.

The frame extends from inside the entrance-hall (see photo, right) to the exposed porch section. In this dry, western environment, wood can be exposed to the weather without much risk of decay.

Hammer-beam roof trusses, such as the one in the foreground, were developed in the Middle Ages to make large spans without supporting columns or long timbers. One probable reason for their development was the lack of long timbers—most of Europe's virgin forests had been harvested by the 12th century. Hammer beams were usually ornately carved and molded, making this one a subtle echo of its medieval archetype.

size
5,200 sq. ft.

completed
1992

location
Central Montana

Banked into the side of a hill, the house cascades down with the terrain, from the garage to the main living level. To keep the first-floor level open, the ground floor is used for additional bedrooms and a recreation area. The cross-gabled entry roof timbers do not join at the intersection but rather weave by one another.

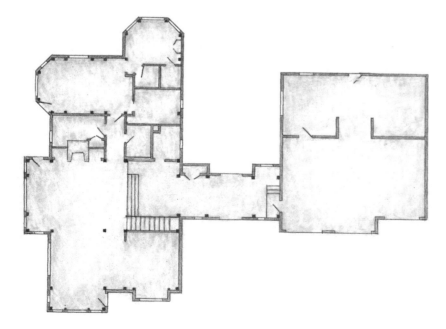

left Built with timber salvaged from the Long-Bell mill, the frame was rich with quality and character from the beginning. Molding and carving details enhance the elegance, while large timbers, extra bracing, and rugged joinery make the structure sturdy enough to withstand the region's snow and wind loads.

Cross-bracing, or scissors bracing, has the effect of bringing the high ceiling down in the dining area, while still leaving the space vaulted. The braces also bring great lateral strength to the structure. The fir roof boards got a light whitewash to brighten their color.

High ceilings do more than enlarge spaces; combined with tall windows, they allow light to penetrate more deeply into the living spaces and open up views of the sky, trees, and mountains. The owner can check out skiing conditions while still in bed. The frame not only holds up the house but also defines zones and frames interior spaces. Even the bed's headboard is directly attached to the posts.

*No money is better spent
than what is laid out for domestic satisfaction.*
—Samuel Johnson

Western Chateau

Tops of buildings are "peaks," the continuous crest is a "ridge," and the low-lying creases between roof slopes are "valleys." Much of the language of architecture grew out of nature, and it follows that good design "learns" from its natural context. In a mountain setting, the appropriate building geometry mimics the terrain. This home is hunkered into a mountainside at nearly 10,000 ft. For many years the site was a pastureland for sheep, and it is still visited more by elk than by people. Though of grand quality, the architectural intent was to blend, because the most magnificent thing about this home is its spectacular setting.

Height restrictions forced second-floor spaces to fit snugly under the roofline, but adding dormers to the individual rooms solved the problem, bringing in light, ventilation, headroom, and emergency egress.

A projecting gable bay extends the great room just enough to allow traffic flow around the furniture, while interior posts anchor and loosely define spatial boundaries. Large interior braces give the lateral strength needed for this wall of glass. The window wall is specifically organized so that each unit fits tightly between the posts and beams of the framework. It's not as simple to achieve as it looks. Either frame-opening dimensions determine custom window sizes or standard window sizes determine opening dimensions—either way there's no room for error.

size
5,600 sq. ft.

completed
1996

location
Southern Colorado

Though the frame encloses a considerable volume, its configuration is straightforward: Common rafters bear on a central wall, extending to exterior plates. Cross-gables and dormers break up the roofline and extend the interior spaces. Rooms and living areas tend to follow the patterns articulated by the frame, but there are no strict rules. The timber positions are fixed, but the defined boundaries are elastic.

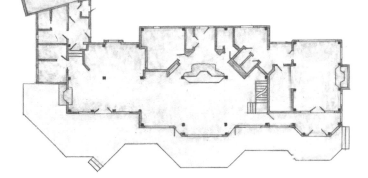

In this open arrangement, the kitchen is the command post and a common gathering place. A raised counter provides visual separation and serves as an informal eating bar. The "formal" dining room is directly to the right; the small breakfast table (photo at left) is in the next bay, and the great room is in the bay beyond, defined by the interior posts. From the kitchen, one can survey it all.

Salvaged fir timbers and southern pine flooring are remnants of the early industrial revolution. Recycling wooden building materials is not only responsible but also brings a level of quality not readily available from today's forests. Generally, there is more heartwood in the slow-growing virgin timber, which enhances color, texture, and strength.

Frame details are simply expressed, and the timber edges are only lightly chamfered. This restraint helps to retain the utilitarian heritage of the timbers' earlier industrial life in mill buildings. Metal stains, nail holes, and other "defects" are evidence of this former life.

Exterior decks, typically of poor design and minimal structure, have ruined the appearance of many a fine building. With large limestone pillars and heavily built railings, this home doesn't fall into that trap.

To anyone who has lived in a timberframe home, the typical American bedroom has the look and feel of a shoebox. In this room, by contrast, exposed timbers lend an air of natural beauty and add texture to surfaces and edges. Framed without timbers, the dormer is a spatial counterpoint and this room's lightwell.

left The home's insulating system wraps the timberframe in a thick blanket of unbroken, rigid insulation, so lofty spaces don't lose heat to the upper regions. Iron grilles for the railing came from a dismantled New Orleans building, and an old, refurbished iron light fixture of a similar style continues the period influence. But enough iron and wood: A beautifully crafted, pure white cast fireplace is a bold and contrasting feature.

No space is wasted in good timberframe design. The most interesting areas are often those tucked under sloping rooflines. By organizing storage and counters at the low eaves, it's possible to use all floor space productively and still have full headroom where necessary.

Light and space are the hallmarks of modern timberframe design. This solarium is actually a hallway, which allows natural light and heat to spill into the master bedroom to the left. Windows and doors are simply trimmed with wood at their head and sill, but the sides are trimless with rounded plaster corners.

There is nothing lavish about this space, except that the entire built volume is visible. If exposing it all seems an extravagance, losing it would be a waste. Here, the window and door openings are framed only with plaster, which serves to accentuate the timberframe.

The house is more than a box within which to live; it is a soul activity to be retrieved from the numbness of the world of modern objects.
—Robert Sardello, *Facing the World with Soul*

Chalet West

The archetype of mountain architecture is the chalet. In the alpine regions of Switzerland, Germany, and Austria, broad-gabled buildings with huge sheltering roofs have been the vernacular style for hundreds of years, suggesting that the proper design in the mountains is mountain-like. The owners of this home had traveled extensively in Switzerland and were unequivocal about their desire to bring the chalet style to their mountain site in Montana. But the traditional influence only prevailed on the exterior; the interior was opened to space and light in the manner of contemporary timberframe homes.

The big, overhanging roof protecting an exterior balcony, the carved newels and balusters, and the course-textured siding all add to the chalet's authenticity. What is most authentic, though, is the timberframe, which was the structural system historically used for this type of building.

Structural timbers frame the tiled chimney. While the upper beam doubles as the loft railing, cherry splines pass through the braces and give support to the loft floor where it wraps around the chimney. The ruddy tones of the tile complement the natural color of the salvaged fir timbers and emphasize the pleasingly simple lines of the chimney.

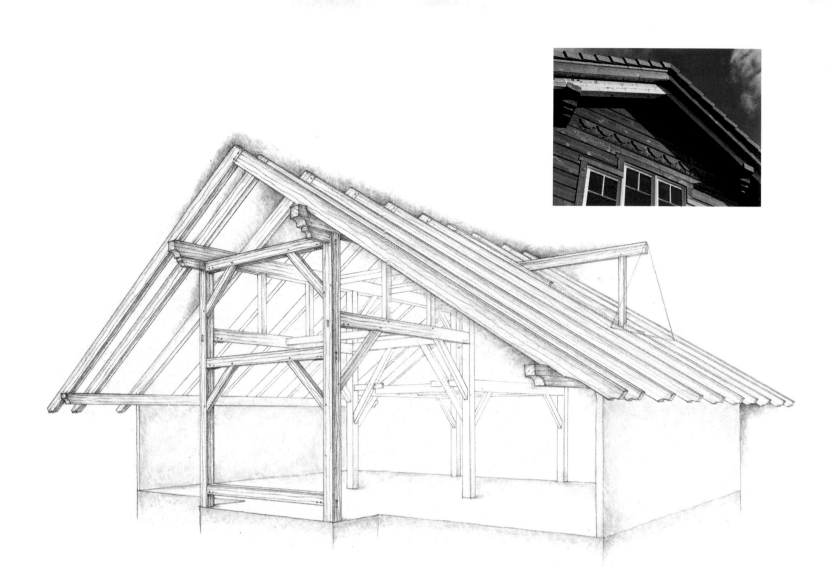

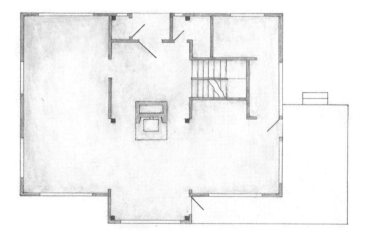

size
3,200 sq. ft.

completed
1995

location
Central Montana

Parallel with the ridgeline, the frame forms three aisle spaces and two perpendicular bays. Within such basic grids, there are numerous organizational possibilities. In this plan, primary areas face the south-side views, a work center is in the second-floor loft, and secondary spaces and bedrooms are on the north side and in a ground-floor level. Exterior walls below the eaves are conventionally framed.

From the loft level, you can see through the upper gable windows to the southern view. Though there isn't a great deal of south-facing glass, there's enough to provide passive solar heating on sunny days.

below The gable's broad face and the projecting roof define the chalet style. Upper timbers extend to support the outermost rafters. Chinked horizontal planks, with an occasional carved layer, make a unique siding with an old-world appearance.

left Because the primary living areas are open, the cherry cabinets and granite countertops play an important interior design role as partitions. Exterior posts and braces can be difficult to work around in a kitchen (upper cabinets and shelving tend to get in the way), so the timber-frame does not extend to the side walls, which are conventional construction.

*Isn't it true that a pleasant house makes winter
more poetic, and doesn't winter add to the poetry of a house?*
—Thomas De Quincey

Snow Barn

Timeless integrity in architecture can be elusive. Passing fancies often prevail, and there's usually an attempt by the designer to achieve too much. As naturalist John Burroughs suggested, the biggest pitfall of all is lack of humility: "Pride, when it is conscious of itself, is death to the nobly beautiful, whether in dress, manners, equipage,

or house-building." The owners of this home wanted a solid, comfortable, low-maintenance dwelling, with an uncomplicated design. Timberframe barns are a significant part of Vermont's farming heritage, so a timberframe barn home was a simple and appropriate solution.

Classic New England barns have consistent shapes for a simple reason: Farmers aren't big on pretense. Make a house like a barn and the style is practical and frugal.

(PHOTOS BY TEDD BENSON/BRIAN SMELTZ)

Kitchen and dining areas are defined by their open timber spaces. The timberframe is constructed with Port Orford cedar, a wood revered by Japanese temple builders for its beauty, strength, weather resistance, and workability. Hardwood splines, used to strengthen the connections, are left exposed to celebrate the joints.

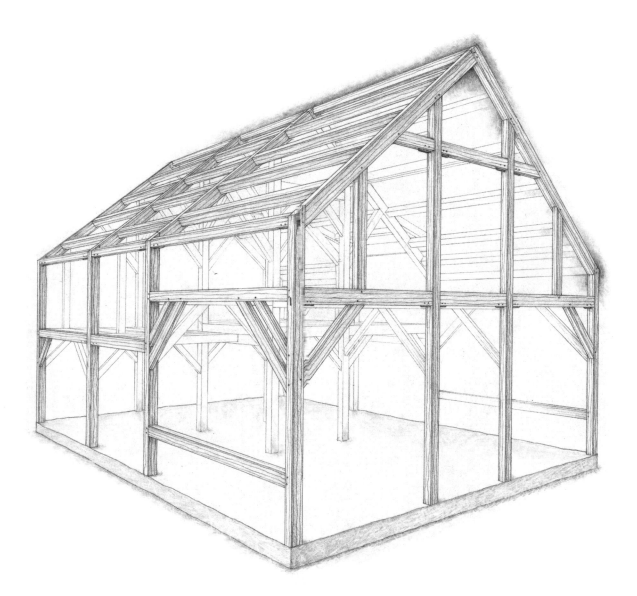

size
2,500 sq. ft.

completed
1993

location
Northwest Vermont

"The lesson for the ages from three-aisled structures is that columns articulate space in a way that makes people feel comfortable making and remaking walls and rooms anchored to the columns" (Stewart Brand, *How Buildings Learn*). *Four simple bents, or frame cross sections, divide the interior spaces into a series of defined spaces with more potentials than restraints. This elementary grid has been the basis for countless unique homes throughout the world. Inspired by barn interiors, there are several ceiling heights.*

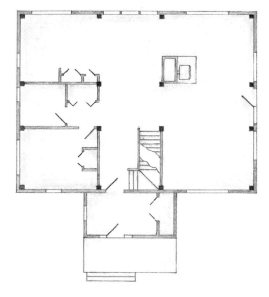

Sunlight streams through the space from tall doors and high windows on the opposite wall. In the background, expressive through-tenon joints for joists double as support shelves for laminated stair stringers.

above right A loft over the high-ceilinged living room serves as a home office and study area. The master bedroom is on a lower level at the far end.

left The craft of timberframing is all about strong, tight-fitting joints. Here, walnut wedges secure a tenon (and add contrast to the light-colored, soft-textured Port Orford cedar).

right Although barnlike from the outside, the interior is rich with timber details and a variety of spaces. In the entryway, the ceiling height drops to the lowest of its three levels. Wedged stair treads echo the timberframe joinery.

Light, God's eldest daughter, is a principal beauty in a building.
—Thomas Fuller, English cleric

Sun Lodge

In the mountains of southern Colorado, there is little precedent for residential architecture. For the Native Americans, the elevation was too high for settlement. And when the miners came for gold and silver, all their energy was directed into the earth; little is left of what they built above ground. Those who design and build in this region must therefore be aware that the building archetypes for the future are being created today. With the ever-present sun, the magnificent views, and the rugged

terrain as inspiration, and a timberframe at its core, this home's design is a bold and appropriate stride in the right direction.

Cutting into a hillside site created a protected area for the building, which is oriented to capture the panoramic views to the south. The north-side entry faces onto an interior courtyard.

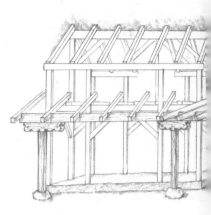

More than just a vaulted space, the great room is a stunning hall of light. High windows and lofty spaces allow the light to penetrate deep into the home. Roof extensions and conventionally framed bays not only make cozy alcoves, but their projected sides also bring morning and evening sunlight into the great room space.

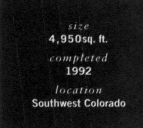

size
4,950 sq. ft.

completed
1992

location
Southwest Colorado

Three independent frames, with conventionally framed connections and bay extensions, make up the building's primary structure. Salvaged fir timbers were used in the central frame, while the outer wings are made with new fir. The porch timbers were sandblasted to make them look older. The round columns, which once were pillars in the Boston College ice arena, are longleaf southern pine. Porch plates, rafters, and column capitals are salvaged fir.

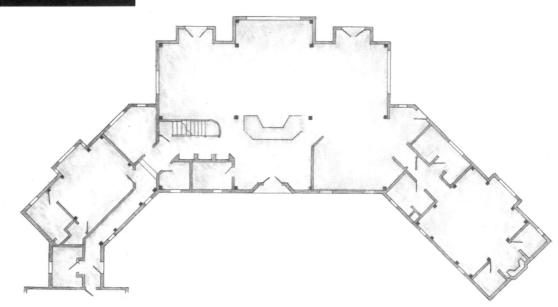

An oak spline, connecting to a beam on the opposite side, is extended to add strength to the joint. Its carved end is both decorative and structural.

left A well-built stone chimney brings with it the rugged textures and mottled coloration that are the real stuff of the earth; as with natural timber, imitation always fails.

The Southwest design influence is evident in the extended log joists, the arched cavities between them, the rounded corners, the geometric pattern on the balusters, and the rustic post and capital detail on the porch. Timberframing is an elemental and adaptable building system. It doesn't dictate design style.

Soft-textured timbers and the planked ceiling create an elaborate wooden canopy over the white plaster walls and the light-filled space of the master bedroom. It's hard to imagine the proportions of the room working without the timbers, which add texture and lower the volume to a comfortable level.

Timbers anchor and frame an extended bay, which is this bedroom's natural light and ventilation source. It's also an inviting window seat for reading, soaking in a little sunlight, or just enjoying the view.

left A second-floor bedroom fits snugly under the sloping roof. There is a both a sense of enclosure and spaciousness as the room rises from the low eaves to the ridge beam. A gable dormer lifts the exterior wall high enough for full-height windows and creates added headroom.
(PHOTO BY TEDD BENSON)

right Twig shutters and a bentwood sink base are fine examples of the owners' inspired decorating abilities. While an interior decorator can help, interior design is one area where homeowners can really make a difference. It's what makes the home personal.

...do you know that it's possible (although very, very hard) to create a building that makes you feel the way you do when a loved one smiles at you or when a child holds your hand?
—David M. Foley, designer

Mining Hall

You don't have to go far up into the mountains west of Denver before you come upon the last built vestiges of the region's mining era. The first mining-town homes were often nothing more than canvas tents; most of those made of wood were temporary shacks, little better than wooden tents. The best-quality construction was reserved for the mine buildings themselves, which were rugged structures built with heavy timbers and logs. This Colorado home was inspired by that sturdy and hopeful mining architecture, not by the houses that went up during the gold rush. Its other significant influence is the modern timberframe hall.

Among its many functions, an entryway needs to serve as a transition, to give a sense of the home and its organization without revealing it all.

(PHOTOS BY TEDD BENSON)

A successful home design has small nooks and alcoves to augment the larger living spaces. If convenient to the kitchen, a cozy eating corner is likely to see more use than a large dining room, simply because its intimate scale is appealing for small groups or for solo dining. Salvaged fir ceiling timbers extend to conventionally framed walls.

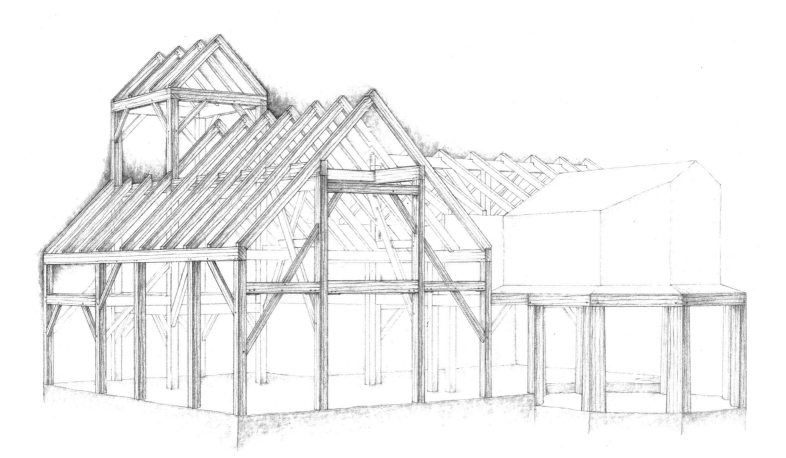

size
4,400 sq. ft.

completed
1994

location
Colorado

Employing several hybrid construction techniques and anchored by the open-timber-roofed great room, this home uses timberframing to good advantage. One wing of the house has roof and floor construction tied into conventionally framed walls, and the room over the octagon dining room has no timberframing. Salvaged fir timbers, mostly from the Long-Bell mill, are used in the primary living areas and left exposed.

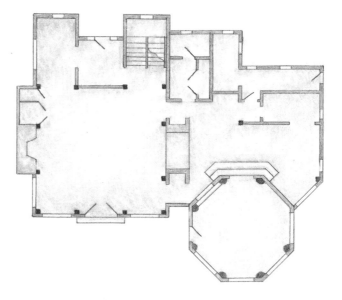

Large salvaged timbers support the elevated bridge, which also creates a convenient port cochere for unloading people or groceries before parking the car. A heavy oak door and thick, natural-edged siding express the rugged simplicity of the design.

left Clearly inspired by the design of mine buildings common to this region, the home has a utilitarian appearance and delightful features. The tower room is designed after a mine building element called a "tipple." The bridge connects the main house to guest bedrooms above the garage.

right Dining can be both rustic and luxurious, when the room is spacious and the view is glorious. Pine log posts encircle the room, echoing the forest setting. Two large, recycled beams orient the room and define a space for the table. The south-facing room receives sunlight throughout the day.

In Addition

A comfortable house
is a great source of
happiness. It ranks
immediately after health
and a good conscience.
—Sydney Smith,
English cleric

Architecture is the reaching out for the truth.
—Louis Kahn, architect

Master's Wing

Norm Abram has had a significant influence on the shaping of our homes. Through his many years as the featured master builder on PBS's *This Old House,* he has become "America's carpenter." In this age of television hype and spin, what is most unusual about Norm is that he is the genuine article: a talented wood craftsman, a knowledgeable builder, and a good spokesman for the woodworking and building trades. It was therefore an honor and a special challenge to be asked to build the timberframe ell for his home. The resulting structure fused fine woodworking with frame carpentry, just as Norm does.

Details: Hand-wrought ironwork and cherry wedges fasten together a confluence of post and truss.

right Sitka spruce was used for the trusses, rafters, ridge, and purlins; Port Orford cedar for the wall plates and posts. Scale and proportion are enhanced by the arched trusses, which seem to pull the ceiling down toward earth.

below Between two television shows and numerous public appearances, Norm's a busy guy. That he still attempts to complete his own finish work is remarkable; that he isn't finished yet should be gratifying to other professional builders with unfinished houses.

The timberframe ell lies between the main house and the garage. It encloses the kitchen and the family room. A wall of south-facing glass, topped by small transom windows, brings light deep into the open space. (PHOTO BY TEDD BENSON)

*I want a house that has got over all its troubles; I don't want to spend
the rest of my life bringing up a young and inexperienced house.*
—Jerome K. Jerome

Abundant Farm

Carved posts at either end of the space
help formalize the timberframe's effect
on the room.

For more than 30 years, the owner lived in the original 1773 timberframe home known locally as "Poor Farm" (see pp. 224-229). She always loved the old house, but it wasn't perfect. Spaces were small and dark, which accentuated winter's dreary effect. Also, the house is located at the dead end of a miles-long dirt road. It gets lonely out there. So the owner decided to build an addition that would do three things: maintain the architectural and structural standards of the old house; give her a spacious, sunlit room to brighten her days; and create a place for large and frequent parties.

above Adding to a stately old colonial home risked harming the building's architectural beauty and integrity. This addition successfully honors the traditional design without disturbing its classic lines. The cutaway corner subtracts space but adds light and interest.

right A truss spans the large, open room. To match the color and texture of the exposed timbers in the old home, the timber-frame was built with salvaged Douglas fir, left with a rough-sawn surface, and stained with a brew of vinegar and rusty nails.

One must remember that there is a difference between a house, a place of shelter, and a home, a place where all your affections are centered.
—Lucy Maynard Simon, *The Domestic Service*

Trumpet Haven

Lives lived large sometimes need large spaces. Overlooking a private pond on a wooded site in northern South Carolina, this country home, unpretentious on the exterior, opens to a large central hall that gives evidence

of big passions and varied interests. The owners are both well-known physicians, people with much experience and accomplishment but with nothing to prove. Their home tells stories of their love of plants, art, and books; of an outdoorsman and many travels; and especially of a love of music and brass musical instruments. It also tells of their love of timber and wood.

The timberframe is built with a mix of species: Salvaged southern pine is predominant, but there is also Douglas fir, Sitka spruce, salvaged chestnut, and incense cedar from the site.

below A 200-year-old hand-hewn chestnut beam still works hard here, supporting a major roof load from the two posts, while throughout the space a world-class collection of trumpets and other brass instruments makes the room a veritable museum.

Valley timbers and a ridge beam converge. Because of the compound angles involved, cutting and laying out joints like these is demanding.

Only the central hall is timber-framed in this Southern "Up Country" style home. The outer service and bedroom wings are framed conventionally. As s often the case in timberframe building, the exterior gives no clue to the dramatic interior.

...buildings give us a way to leave a lasting mark, to conduct a conversation across the generations.
—Michael Pollan, *A Place of My Own*

Barn Anew

The owners had lived comfortably in their 18th-century home for many years, but they knew it was not quite complete. A barn had once been connected to the house in the classic New England style, and it had always seemed

to the owners that without it the house was missing a piece of essential architecture. When they sold their business and retired, they found themselves in a position to build a new home of their dreams. But after much soul-searching, they decided to stay in the old house, replace the missing barn, and build into it the additional spaces they wanted.

It couldn't be simpler—a thick oak beam, a glass bowl, and a faucet against a black backdrop of counter and floor—but it's an artistic touch that turns this utility/bath room into something special.

right Antique Italian furniture has been renovated to become a part of the guest quarters' galley kitchen. The loft provides an additional sitting or sleeping area and connects to the owners' workshop. The shaped pattern of the railing boards is in the Swedish Gustavian style.

The table and "eckbank" (corner bench) were custom-made in Switzerland out of old wood (built-in corners like these are common in Swiss homes). The timberframe is oak, roof boards are white pine, and the floorboards are salvaged southern pine.

The barn banks into a natural slope. Seen from the back side, its upper level is used as an exercise area that contains an outside spa; the guest quarters are to the left.

*Should not every apartment in which man dwells be lofty enough
to create some obscurity overhead, where
flickering shadows may play at evening above the rafters?*
—Henry David Thoreau

Timber Sanctum

It was inevitable: A timber engineer who spends his days designing timberframes wanted more than vicarious pleasure from his work. He would build a timberframe building for himself and his family. Before the situation got dangerous, a class was organized to teach timberframing lessons to paying students, who at the same time would build a new great-room addition to the engineer's existing home. More than 30 students from around the country spent a week cutting and shaping a variety of unique joints on numerous kinds of timber to bring a long-held dream to reality.

Projecting beams at the gables give a hint of what lies behind the unassuming facade. Master stonework is a feature of both the exterior and interior.

above Sitka spruce and laminated fir braces connect to a salvaged fir post. Timber joinery was precisely cut by a group of first-time timber-framing students.

left It's only one room, but it contains salvaged Douglas fir, southern pine, and spruce; redwood rafters reclaimed from wine-tank staves; laminated fir cutoffs from a church truss project; fresh-sawn Port Orford cedar and eastern spruce from the site; oak pegs and splines; and wooden nuts and bolts.

A home is not a mere transient shelter; its essence lies in its permanence, in its capacity of accretion and solidification, in its quality of representing, in all its details, the personalities of the people who live in it.
—H. L. Mencken

Thatched Nest

The timberframe tradition in North America has its roots in England, so it seems fitting that this book should end in that country with this 20th-century barn addition. After more than 300 years of development and a modern timberframe resurgence, we return to Suffolk, East Anglia, the area of England the first colonists came from, with a sample of modern American timberframing.

Though the finish on the timbers is more polished, the timberframe still reveals its English roots and appears quite at home under a traditional thatched roof.

Adding the thatched barn to the property took some doing. The beauty of the English countryside reflects good taste, but it is also carefully controlled. The pink cottage is 18th century; the thatched barn is new.

Thatch, coupled with modern waterproofing techniques, is an effective roofing material, and in England thatching is still a relevant craft. The barn was designed to give the owners a larger space for parties and family gatherings, while also serving as guest quarters and as a service building for the in-ground pool.

right Bedrooms are located at either end of the second floor, tucked under the gabled roof. In modern timberframe design, it is typical to incorporate all the enclosed volume into the living area. White plastered wall and ceiling surfaces help to make the smaller spaces feel light and airy.

left A spacious living room is located in the end of the barn. Douglas fir timbers and a simple, pine-planked ceiling bring warmth to the room. A bridge connects the two second-floor bedrooms.

Epilogue:
In the Past

We shape our

buildings; thereafter

they shape us.

—Winston Churchill

left By the time the virgin forests of the West Coast
were set upon by ax and saw, timberframing had already been replaced
by balloon framing throughout North America.

This soaring room was originally open to the lower level, and smoke from a firepit escaped through exposed roof tiles and gable openings, blackening the timberframe, including its meticulously carved crownpost. The floor and chimney were added in the 1500s.

The timberframe homes featured in this book reflect the technology and taste of our times. Their design and decoration arose from a general evolution of lifestyle and our expectations of comfort as much as from the effect of their geographic setting, climate, and the building system itself. It has always been so. The story of timberframe building is intertwined with the development of the many societies in which it was practiced.

Timberframing dates back several thousand years and has played a major role in the history of residential construction throughout the world. By the Middle Ages, timberframing had become the predominant method of wood frame building. The whole history from prehistoric beginnings to the fabulous luxuries we live with today is too broad and diverse to tell here, so we'll narrow our focus to the roots of the modern timberframe home in North America. We'll trace its evolution from England to North America by visiting three homes—all still in use—whose dates of construction span from the late Middle Ages to the pre-Revolutionary War years in the United States. The newest of the three is 225 years old.

Little Hall

The early history of the home called "Little Hall" is sketchy. It was built in the late Middle Ages in the town of Lavenham, in southwest Suffolk County, England. At the time, few public records were kept, but there is some evidence that the first wing of Little Hall was built in the late 1300s for William Causton, a clothmaker, and that the central hall and the opposite wing were added in the mid-15th century. To give this time period some perspective, recall that Europe was still reeling from the loss of a third of the population inflicted by the Black Death; the Bible had just been translated into English (1382) but wouldn't be in circulation for another 150 years; England's Hundred Years' War with France still raged; the Wars of the Roses were about to get

Continuously occupied for over 600 years, Little Hall absorbed numerous renovations and additions but never lost its medieval essence. It has witnessed a good portion of England's history and weathered vast changes in technology and taste. The yellow ochre paint color is a naturally occurring pigment found in the East Anglia area.

In the 15th century, this room was an open hall, with no flooring, fireplace, glazed windows, or second floor level. There was a dirt floor and, approximately where the table is now placed, a firepit for cooking and heat. Because many people probably lived and worked in this single room, neither privacy nor comfort were considerations.

under way (1455-1485), which would establish the House of Tudor; England was still Catholic; Christopher Columbus had not yet sailed to America; and Chaucer, not Shakespeare, was the bard of England. Little Hall, like many timberframe buildings from that period, has been continuously occupied for over 600 years.

From around 1350 to 1550, Lavenham was a thriving market town and an important center of the cloth industry in England. Even the Wars of the Roses did not dampen its surging prosperity. There was an enormous demand for the blue woolen cloth ("Lavenham Blues") for which Lavenham had become renowned throughout Europe, causing a building boom of homes large and small, several guildhalls, inns, pubs, and a magnificent parish church (see the photos on pp. 216-217). Over the centuries, Lavenham's wealth waned, but its ties to the cloth industry held fast, even during several hundred years of deep recession. As a result, there was little building in Lavenham from the late-17th century through the 19th century, making it one of the most unspoiled medieval towns in Europe. Centuries of prosperity built a village full of magnificent timberframed buildings and centuries of poverty kept them from being ruined by changing fashion.

By the time Little Hall was built, timberframing was highly evolved. Not only were the craftsmen able to mold and shape large timbers into structures of furniture quality and beauty, but they also had developed sophisticated knowledge of timber engineering. Medieval timberframers were responsible for the magnificent open timber roofs of numerous cathedrals and manor halls, in which grand spanning roof systems were also highly decorated with intricate carvings on the timber surfaces. One of the more

Hall houses of the 15th century had standardized layouts. This room is called the "solar" and was located above the buttery and store in one of the cross wings. It was the bedroom for the master's family.

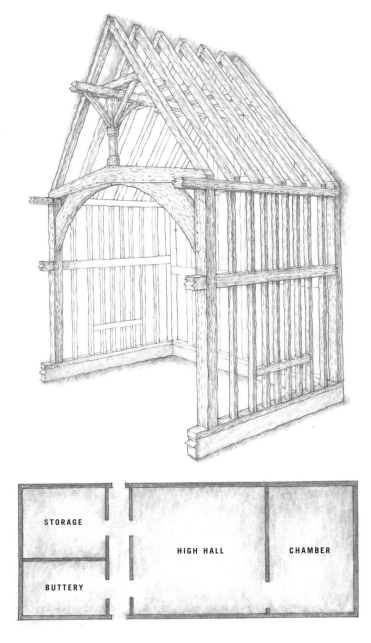

Little Hall's timberframe space was rather majestic, with its high roof, gothic arched braces, and carved crown post. The closely spaced timbers are all oak, but the trees from which most of the timbers were hewn were small and gnarled since England's forests were quite depleted by that time. Hall house plans of the period rarely varied much from the typical plan of two cross-wings sandwiching the central "high hall."

notable examples is London's Westminster Hall, built in the mid-1300s, which has multibracketed roof trusses that span 68 ft. and remains today as a marvel of timber engineering.

A "HALL HOUSE" OF OAK, WATTLE, AND DAUB

The materials used for construction were few and basic. Timberframes were made of oak. Nothing else was considered suitable. Ironically, although the timberframers were at a pinnacle of accomplishment, the wood they had available was of relatively poor quality. England's forest resources had been significantly depleted by the time of Little Hall's construction, which meant that suitable timbers often had to be shipped from distant places and framers had to use pieces that were twisted and crooked. The spaces between the timbers of the frame were filled with either bricks or "wattle and daub." Wattle was a woven lattice of withes, which was covered by layers of daub, consisting of clay, lime, horsehair and cow dung. Roofing was thatch or tile. And in the early 15th century, that's all there was to the building.

Until the end of the 16th century, the "hall house" was a standard for domestic dwellings. The hall itself was just a large open room with exposed rafters. Typically, but not always, two wings flanked the hall. On one side were two utility rooms adjacent to an entry and through-passage; on the other was a chamber used for sleeping. Before later modifications and additions, Little Hall was a slight variation of this basic layout.

The difference between the wealthy and the poor was in the size and height of the halls. We can assume that the Causton family, at least initially, had only modest means. At approximately 18 ft. by 22 ft., "Little Hall" is definitely small. More substantial halls are often 24 ft. by 40 ft., or larger. Still, Little

Hall's timberframe structure is of good quality. The elaborate work on the crown post, tie beam, and arched brackets reveals the work of excellent timber-framers.

But the quality of the craftsmanship belies the kind of life people would have lived in Little Hall. The reason the hall was originally open is that there

The oldest wing of Little Hall is the exposed-timber building to the left, dating from the 1380s. The central hall and the far wing were built early in the 1400s, probably replacing earlier construction.

Alden Spoke

Quite forgetful of self, and full of the praise of his rival / Archly the maiden smiled, and, with eyes overrunning with laughter / Said, in a tremulous voice, "Why don't you speak for yourself, John?" Thus, according to Longfellow's poetic fable, Priscilla Mullins gave John Alden a clue that she was more interested in the messenger than the message he felt obliged to deliver on behalf of Captain Miles Standish. There is more myth than reality in "The Courtship of Miles Standish," but it is fact that Priscilla and John's romance was true and legend-worthy, if only for its context. They met on the Mayflower in 1620 during its voyage from England to America and were the first newlyweds in Plymouth Colony.

John and Priscilla had long and successful lives together. While John was a lifelong leader in colony government, Priscilla managed their household and bore 11 children. Together they built a house and developed property that was destined to be home to generations of Aldens into the 20th century. John and Priscilla were fortunate just to survive. Due to inadequate housing during the first brutal New England winter, fully one-half of the 102 Mayflower passengers died, including Priscilla Mullins' parents and brother. If anybody came with illusions of Utopia, that first winter surely stripped those dreams to the bone. Because decent housing was an essential element in the society they hoped to create, timber-framing played a leading role in the building of early America.

Until the early 20th century, this home was continuously occupied by the Alden family. Over the years, they made few alterations to the original construction, but they did add the paneling and plaster.

Built in 1653, the Alden house is the only remaining house built by a Mayflower Pilgrim. By that time, the hearth was the heart of the home and a modicum of thermal comfort was expected. Clapboards replaced wattle and daub infill due to the harsh New England climate. (PHOTO BY TEDD BENSON)

Most of the colonists came from the southeastern counties of England, where timberframing was by far the predominant building system for residential dwellings. John Alden himself presumably came from the town of Harwich, which is about 30 miles from Lavenham. Clearly, the building traditions and evolutions that built and changed Little Hall were essentially the knowledge that informed America's first house builders. In fact, what the colonists built in early America was nearly identical in structure and style to those they left in England. Little Hall of the early 17th century, with its recent renovation of a hearth and second floor, was basically the dream home in the New World.

One great advantage the Colonial timber-framers had over their peers in England was the abundant virgin forests. Tall, straight trees allowed them to hew timbers to the building's length and height, making the timberframes stiffer and stronger. For example, this nicely shaped and chamfered gunstock post passes from the roof to the foundation.

John and Priscilla's first home in Plymouth was a one-room, windowless timberframed hut, probably with thatched roof and wattle-and-daub chimney. This home may have had wattle-and-daub infilling like those of England, but it was soon discovered that the climate was too harsh for that system. Governor Bradford reported after a winter storm that it "caused much daubing of our houses to fall down." Soon it was the norm to cover the timber-frame with lapped "weatherboards," which we now refer to as clapboards.

ADAPTING TO THE NEW WORLD

In 1627, the Aldens were granted land "on the other side of the bay," which they farmed seasonally be-fore moving there permanently in 1632 along with many other settlers. This was the beginning of Duxborrough town, now known as Duxbury. It was also the beginning of a new era of independence for the colonists. Life in the Plymouth Colony was rigid-ly communal. It was basically an enclosed fort, with small building lots within and an acre for each fami-ly to garden outside of the palisaded village. In Duxbury the Aldens had 100 acres and were free to build a family estate and to prosper by dint of their own "severe effort."

As John and Priscilla contemplated building on their new land in Duxbury, they had been in New England for 12 years. Even by that time, some dis-tinct differences between timberframe homebuilding in England and Early America had begun to emerge.

First, there were the climactic differences that had all but eliminated the wattle-and-daub infilling be-tween timbers. It wasn't just that the winters were far colder and stormier than in England, the sum-mers were also hotter. In Plymouth, England, the av-erage yearly temperature variation between high and

By the late 17th century, there was a higher standard for personal comfort and a greater sensitivity regarding privacy. Alden's 1653 house almost certainly had a private bedchamber for John and Priscilla, which was rare only a century earlier.

The second-floor workroom, located above the kitchen in the rear of the house, reveals how the entire house was originally finished. Vertical pine planking was attached to the outside of the timberframe, serving as a nailbase for the exterior clapboards and as interior finish.

low is 63°F, while in Plymouth, Massachusetts, it is 110°F. Along with the temperature variance comes a significant change in relative humidity, which causes wood and other materials to shrink and swell and also induces rot more quickly. It wasn't long before John Alden and the other colonists learned that it was more practical to cover the timberframe with a protective, weatherproof skin of overlapped boards and to refrain from exposing frame members to the weather at eave and gable roof overhangs. They

were also learning that the shallow foundations (1-ft. to 2-ft. depth) common in England did not suffice when the soil freezes as far down as 4 ft.

BUILDING WITH BETTER MATERIALS AND METHODS

Two significant differences in the New World allowed carpenters to make some structural improvements over the Old World timberframes. Oak was still the wood of choice, as it had been in England, but the trees of the virgin New England forests grew tall and straight, while English carpenters struggled to make decent buildings out of depleted and scraggly forest resources.

In the New World, designs began to include timbers that spanned the entire length, width, and height of the building, rather than short timbers punctuated by beams and posts. In New England, although professionals were hired to design and prepare the timbers, raisings were generally accomplished by community work parties.

Early colonial homes were direct derivatives of the late medieval architecture in England—but stripped of ornamentation. Puritan settlers, in fact, disdained distinctions of class and strove for homes that were merely "faire and pleasant." "Faire" implied durable and well ordered, which was manifest in massive timberframes with little elaboration and exteriors that were honest expressions of the interior layout and the structural requirements. A building such as Lavenham's Guildhall would not have been appreciated in the colonies.

The first home built by the Aldens in Duxbury was a significant improvement over the primitive hut they left at Plymouth, but it was still small—only 10½ ft. by 38 ft.—and of a fairly typical "long house" configuration. It is easy to imagine that shelter was only one of the pressing matters facing the Aldens on their new land. Beside the necessities of farming and putting up food, John Alden also had to help others in the building of their homes, and because he was the assistant to the governor, he had to travel frequently. His house had three rooms in the main floor: a large central kitchen and work room, a "buttery" at one end, and a small bedroom on the other. The second floor might have had an open loft

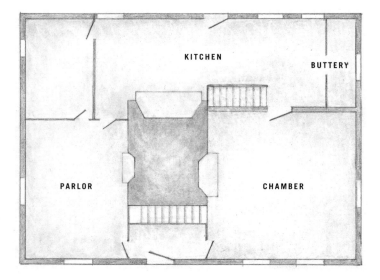

The floor plan has two parts. The back section is actually the Alden's 1628 house moved to the new foundation and added to the new (1653) hall and parlor layout. This two room configuration, with the added rear kitchen, is very common in early colonial building.

or a couple of bedrooms. For John, Priscilla, and as many as nine children, this was home.

BUILDING ON A NEW FOUNDATION

The Aldens prospered on their farm and eventually were able to build a larger home. It was usual to add to the original house as needs and means increased, but John Alden did it differently. He found a new site and constructed a proper foundation there. Then he moved the old house to that location and incorporated it into the construction of the larger home. The first home had been built on a thin stone foundation, which inevitably led to a freezing cold, constantly undulating floor and rapidly rotting sills. This was a practical move. He salvaged the earlier construction, while also building an enduring home that he could pass on to future generations. The new home was completed in 1653.

Like most 17th-century American homes, the Alden house timberframe was intended to be visible to the home's interior. The timbers were carefully finished, with chamfered edges and elegant shaping of gunstocked posts. The frame was enclosed with vertical pine planking, which served as both exterior sheathing and interior finish. Flooring was wide pine boards. In the middle of the home was a huge brick masonry mass that housed four fireplaces, three on the first floor and one on the second.

The room layout of the new house was simple. Four rooms were added to the home, two up and two down. The primary room downstairs was the hall, which was the most important room in the home, as it had been before the advent of the chimney in medieval England. This was the center of family activities. The parlor, on the side of the chimney, was reserved for more formal occasions, was used less frequently, and therefore was smaller. Upstairs were bedrooms, referred to as "chambers," and designated as hall chamber and parlor chamber. When John Alden's family was there, these chambers were packed with beds and children. John and Priscilla lived out their lives in that house and were married for 60 years. The home he built has been owned only by generations of Aldens since. Along the way, the interior of the house was plastered, painted, and paneled, but the house is otherwise much the same as it was when it was built by a man and a woman who arrived on the Mayflower to an unknown world with hopes, dreams, and young love.

Poor Farm

When Nathaniel Sleeper built his central New Hampshire home in 1773, the landscape of colonial America had changed considerably from the time John Alden's house was built a century earlier. The population had swelled to nearly 1.5 million, and the land was being quickly carved up as the settlers pushed north, south, and west. As the land was settled, the dense forests were cleared for farmland. Nature was being tamed and the "errand into the wilderness" seemed less forbidding. Homes were no longer seen as a fortress against a hostile environment.

Although the English were still predominant, there were now immigrants from nearly all the European countries. This great amalgamation was bringing with it changes in architecture and construction methodology. Especially influential were the Dutch in the New York area and the Germans in Pennsylvania, both of whom came to America with long histories of timberframing and who brought advanced skills and unique perspectives.

There was also a war brewing. In Sleeper's neighborhood, there had been a revolt against the "Pine Tree Law" just a year before his house was built. This law, which had been in effect for 50 years, decreed that all pine trees over 12 in. in diameter were reserved for the Royal Navy. There were severe penalties for owners who cut pine trees on their own land. This insidious law was particularly irksome in

When the Revolutionary War began, this home was three years old. One imagines the owners, gathered with neighbors and kin around this very fireplace, planning their participation in the raging battles in Massachusetts. (PHOTO BY TEDD BENSON/BRIAN SMELTZ)

In the 18th century, the most important room in the house was still called the "hall," long after it had lost its medieval appearance and purpose. In this hall, the timber-frame has been completely covered with plaster and paneling and its low ceiling makes it easier to heat, despite the lack of insulation. (PHOTO BY TEDD BENSON/BRIAN SMELTZ)

places where pine was the most abundant species and was needed for construction. When sheriffs tried to enforce the law by arresting and jailing a flagrant violator, 30 men with blackened faces arrived to free the prisoner and the hapless law officers were tarred, feathered, and "ridden on a rail."

There doesn't appear to be any pine in the Sleeper timberframe, but plenty was used for the paneling, sheathing, and flooring, much of it well over 12 in. wide. Perhaps Sleeper thought he was safe from scrutiny in his remote location or perhaps he was flaunting his offense. Whichever the case, his sympathies were not with the British. The New Hampshire Minutemen were among the first to join the fight at Concord and Lexington, and it is likely that Nathaniel and his brother Benjamin were among them. They both fought through the war, even though the battles never came to New Hampshire soil, and Nathaniel's wartime rifle still hangs above the fireplace in his home.

LOOKING OUT ON A NEW WORLD

Sleeper's home is remarkably similar to the John Alden house. This is not just coincidence. Home designs were quite vernacular in a time when security was in the land. Barns were more important than houses and often were built first. The house was a practical necessity and not a place to squander excessive time and resources. Like the Alden house, Sleeper built a three-bay timberframe structure with a huge central chimney flanked by a hall and parlor in the front and a kitchen in the rear. Also like the Alden house, an ell was added later, expanding the kitchen, pantry, and storage. The fireplaces were shallower than the Aldens' and provided more heat. People now expected their homes to provide warmth and more physical comfort.

The later improvements of the Alden house had become common expectations during construction of the Sleeper home and were built into it. Walls were plastered, and there was elegant raised paneling at the hearths. Good-quality glass was more widely available, and the Sleeper house incorporated as much as possible. Large windows had become very popular not only because they let in light, but also because it was now possible to see through the glass (as a result of developments in the glass manufacturing process). It appears that Sleeper even positioned the house to capture a 180° panoramic view of lakes and hills, an idea that would not have meant much in the earlier era when houses typically had only a few panes of distorted blown glass.

Like many early homes, Poor Farm faces south for passive solar benefits. It also captures a 180° panoramic view. By the time this home was built, visibility through glass had been greatly improved, and glass had also become much less expensive, which led to more and larger windows.

(PHOTO BY TEDD BENSON/BRIAN SMELTZ)

In the back room of the house, the timbers are still exposed but the rough finish and minimal shaping suggest that the timberframe was not intended to have aesthetic value in the home. With that attitude prevailing, timberframing was doomed to be replaced by any method that would be quicker and cheaper.

(PHOTO BY TEDD BENSON/BRIAN SMELTZ)

When the Sleeper house was built, "house-joiners," or timberframers, were very much in demand. It is likely that it was difficult to find an experienced carpenter in the far reaches of New Hampshire. Still, the Sleeper timberframe shows professional skill, with excellent hewing of the major timbers and tight joinery throughout. Most of the smaller timbers were sawn, giving evidence that there must have been a sawmill nearby. But the overall appearance of the frame suggests that much of it was not intended to be visible, but rather covered with plaster. This subtle change in the function of the timberframe was the beginning of the end of the dominance of timberframing. When the timberframe was no longer appreciated for its aesthetic value, it was doomed to be replaced by any system that required less time and skill.

After Nathaniel Sleeper's death in 1821, the house received almost no maintenance or attention for more than 100 years. That it survived is remarkable. It is yet another story of impoverishment as the basis for preservation. In the middle 1800s, there was a mass exodus from New England with the discovery of the flat, rich, rockless soil of the Midwest. In 1849, the Sleeper homestead was sold to the town to be used as the Poor Farm. It served that purpose for nearly 40 years and subsequently received little attention from its owners until after World War II. It exists now with its original construction and finishes nearly perfectly preserved—yet another testament to the durability of well-crafted timberframe construction.

It is truly remarkable how close the Sleeper floor plan is to the Alden plan. Many variations were possible, but function was what really mattered, not innovation.

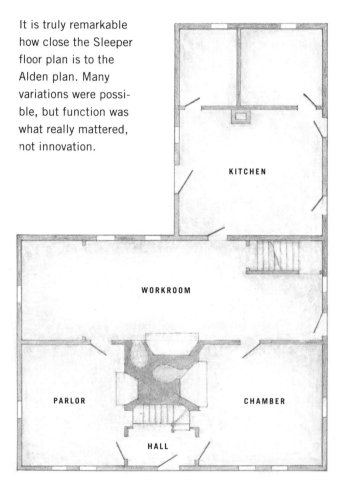

The second-floor parlor chamber is finished in very much the same style as the original Alden house. When the home was built, using these wide pine paneling boards was illegal.

(PHOTO BY TEDD BENSON/BRIAN SMELTZ)

In Conclusion

In the Victorian era, most of the old timberframe homes were renovated to remove evidence of the structure. Gunstock corner posts were chopped away; massive summer beams were encased in plaster; the building's bones were deemed unsightly. This decorative "cleansing" was coincident with the development of the wire nail, the circular saw mill, and the rapid expansion westward. Homes needed to be built quickly and timberframing was simply an obstacle to progress. Stud framing soon took over and by the late 1800s had totally displaced timberframing in residential construction. Aside from a few isolated religious communities, timberframing was discarded in North America until its resurgence in the early 1970s.

Acknowledgments

I express my deepest gratitude to the people whose hard work, patient assistance, encouragement, and tolerance made this book possible: Jamie Salomon and Norm Hersom for the excellent photography and the good times we had traveling together; Sheila Albere, for her diligent and professional assistance and her good cheer throughout the project; Randall Walter, for producing the three-dimensional frame drawings from inadequate information; Kathy Bray for turning these drawings into works of art; Brian Smeltz, for his good advice on many matters and for helping with photography; Marilyn Taggart (one of three wonderful sisters), for helping with the research about the Long-Bell mill; John Baker, of Beeton and Lennard, Ltd., for guiding me around England and leading me to Lavenham; and Renée Attew, for her hospitality during our visit to Little Hall.

I am also very thankful to the staff at Taunton Press. They are a fine team of talented people who are capable of wresting a good book from even the most bullheaded author. I am in their debt: Peter Chapman, Steve Culpepper, Carol Kasper, Carol Singer, and Paula Schlosser.

The true heroes of this book are the people who built the wonderful houses and additions that are featured in these pages. I thank all of them for their faith and vision and for allowing us to appreciate their creations. They are: Norm Abram, Connie and Kurt Bierkan, Hope Birsh and Stephen Plakatoris, Dr. Andrea Branch and David Elliman, Ben Brungraber, Kevin and Mary Grace Burke, Charles and Peggy Carswell, Harriet T. Cope, Lucy and Stewart Evans, Marla Felcher and Max Bazerman, P. E. and Joel Feldman, Austin and Leslie Furst, Robert and Sally Gillespie, Dennis and Eunice Guentzel, Sandra and John Hedlund, Rob and Scottie Held, Dr. Rusty and Kim Hilliard, Michael and Lisa Kittredge, Dr. and Mrs. Steven Leyland, Chuck and Marcia Raches, Michael and Maureen Ruettgers, Tom and Lucy Rutherford, Peter and Carol Sellon, Drew and Lynn Thorburn, Trailsend Ranch, Drs. Joe and Joella Utley, Thomas H. Wake, Angelika Weller, Lynn and Barbara Wickwire, and Gregory Whitehead and Lillian Lennox Whitehead.

I want to extend special thanks to the people in my company, affectionately known as the Beam Team. They spoil me every day with their dedication to the highest standards of product, service, and teamwork. I just cheer. I especially need to acknowledge and thank our design and engineering team for their splendid creations: Ben Brungraber, Tom Goldschmid, Bill Holtz, Brian Smeltz, and Randall Walter. The alumni designers who worked on some of these homes are Tafi Brown, Liz Calabrese, Paul Irwin, AnnMarie Rizzuto, and Andrea Warchaizer.

And finally, my wife, Christine, for her support, encouragement, tolerance, and love. You have my love too, and I will now stop using the dining room table as my office.

Credits

In the Country

Prairie Prospect
(pp. 18-25)
ARCHITECT/DESIGNER
Bensonwood Homes
224 Pratt Road
Alstead, NH 03602
(603) 835-6391
www.bensonwood.com
BUILDER
Johnson & Assoc., Inc.
Lanny Johnson
612 W. 25th Street
Kearney, NE 68847
(308) 234-5983
TIMBERFRAMER
Benson Woodworking Co., Inc.
224 Pratt Road
Alstead, NH 03602
(603) 835-6391

Home Spirit *(pp. 26-31)*
ARCHITECT/DESIGNER
Bensonwood Homes
BUILDER
Owner
TIMBERFRAMER
Benson Woodworking

Craftsman's Way
(pp. 32-37)
ARCHITECT/DESIGNER
The Johnson Partnership
P.O. Box 51133
Seattle, WA 98115
(206) 523-1618
BUILDER
Cascade Joinery
1330 E. Hemmi Road
Everson, WA 98247
(360) 398-8013
TIMBERFRAMER
Cascade Joinery

England West *(pp. 38-45)*
ARCHITECT/DESIGNER
Bensonwood Homes
BUILDER
Benson Woodworking
TIMBERFRAMER
Benson Woodworking

Concord Barn *(pp. 46-51)*
ARCHITECT/DESIGNER
Design Associates
432 Columbia Street
Cambridge, MA 02141
(617) 661-9082
BUILDER
Silva Brothers Construction
41 Locust Street
Reading, MA 01867
(781) 944-3462
TIMBERFRAMER
Timber Framers Guild
of North America
P.O. Box 60, Becket, MA 01223
(888) 453-0879
www.tfguild.org

Vaulted Dwelling
(pp. 52-57)
ARCHITECT/DESIGNER
Bensonwood Homes
BUILDER
Murphy & Furman, Inc.
P.O. Box 2483,
Framingham, MA 01703
(508) 879-5534
TIMBERFRAMER
Benson Woodworking

Time Crafted *(pp. 58-67)*
ARCHITECT/DESIGNER
Dewing and Schmid
146 Mount Auburn Street
Cambridge, MA 02138
(617) 876-0066
BUILDER
J. W. Adams Construction, Inc.
142 Farmers Cliff Road
Concord, MA 01742
(508) 371-0007
TIMBERFRAMER
Benson Woodworking

Horse Haven *(pp. 68-73)*
ARCHITECT/DESIGNER
Bensonwood Homes
BUILDER
Blackhorse Construction
4402 Crompton Court
White Hall, MD 21161
(410) 557-9319
TIMBERFRAMER
Benson Woodworking

On the Water

Timber Bonded
(pp. 76-83)
ARCHITECT/DESIGNER
Scott Ford, in association with
Bensonwood Homes
BUILDER
Benson Woodworking
TIMBERFRAMER
Benson Woodworking

Light Hall *(pp. 84-89)*
ARCHITECT/DESIGNER
Hollis-Crocker Architects, P.C.
1855 E. Main Street, Suite 400
Spartanburg, GA 29307
(864) 583-5296
BUILDER
Foys Construction, Denton Foy
138 Glen Eagles Road
Campobella, SC 29322
(864) 468-5460
TIMBERFRAMER
Benson Woodworking

Island Sentinel
(pp. 90-97)
ARCHITECT/DESIGNER
Milton Rowland and Associates
15 Commercial Wharf
Nantucket, MA 02554
(508) 228-2044

BUILDER
Hill Construction Co., Inc.
4 South Mill Street
Nantucket, MA 02554
(508) 228-3360
TIMBERFRAMER
Benson Woodworking

World Apart *(pp. 98-107)*
ARCHITECT/DESIGNER
Bensonwood Homes
BUILDER
Benson Woodworking,
in association with Sound
Builders, Andy Drakos
517 High Street
Mystic, CT 06355
(860) 536-8276
TIMBERFRAMER
Benson Woodworking

Tree House *(pp. 108-115)*
ARCHITECT/DESIGNER
Bensonwood Homes
BUILDER
Benson Woodworking, in associa-
tion with John McLean, Builder
P.O. Box 1285
Ashland, NH 03217
(603) 968-3254; and Richard
Benton, Jr., Builder
154 Schoolhouse Road
Center Sandwich, NH 03227
(603) 284-6860
TIMBERFRAMER
Benson Woodworking

On Rocks *(pp. 116-121)*
ARCHITECT/DESIGNER
Bensonwood Homes
BUILDER
Blaise Donnelly
46 Lakeside Road
Lakeside, CT 06758
(860) 567-3716
TIMBERFRAMER
Benson Woodworking

Glass Bunker
(pp. 122-129)
ARCHITECT/DESIGNER
Blue Sky Design
Hornby Island, British Columbia
Canada V0R 1Z0
(250) 335-0115
BUILDER
Pacific Wind Construction,
Alan Fletcher, Victoria, B.C.
(250) 388-9143
Tony Meek (interior)
Saltspring Island, B.C.
(250) 746-7257
TIMBERFRAMER
Cascade Joinery

Bras d'Or Ark
(pp. 130-137)
ARCHITECT/DESIGNER
Bensonwood Homes, in associa-
tion with Ron LeLievre, AIA
28 Prospect Street
New Glasgow, Nova Scotia
Canada B2H 4B6
BUILDER
Kavic Construction Co., Ltd.
Gary Wilneff
28 Gordon Avenue
Sydney, Nova Scotia
Canada B1M 1A6
TIMBERFRAMER
Benson Woodworking

In the Mountains

High Plains Salvage
(pp. 140-147)
ARCHITECT/DESIGNER
Big Timberworks
216 N. Church Street
Bozeman, MT 59715
(406) 763-4639
BUILDER
Big Timberworks
TIMBERFRAMER
Big Timberworks

Mountain Manor
(pp. 148-153)
ARCHITECT/DESIGNER
Bensonwood Homes
BUILDER
Tolefson Builders
624 S. 3rd Street
Bozeman, MT 59715
(406) 582-8952
TIMBERFRAMER
Benson Woodworking

Western Chateau
(pp. 154-163)
ARCHITECT/DESIGNER
Bensonwood Homes
BUILDER
Kent Building Co.
307 Society Drive, Suite B
Telluride, CO 81435
(970) 728-3381
TIMBERFRAMER
Benson Woodworking

Chalet West
(pp. 164-169)
ARCHITECT/DESIGNER
Bensonwood Homes
BUILDER
Tolefson Builders
TIMBERFRAMER
Benson Woodworking

Snow Barn *(pp. 170-175)*
ARCHITECT/DESIGNER
Bensonwood Homes
BUILDER
Sisler Builders, Inc.
1885 Barnes Hill Road
Waterbury, VT 05677
(802) 244-5672
TIMBERFRAMER
Benson Woodworking

Sun Lodge *(pp. 176-185)*
ARCHITECT/DESIGNER
Bensonwood Homes
BUILDER
Kent Building Co.
TIMBERFRAMER
Benson Woodworking, in associa-
tion with Timbercraft Homes
85 Martin Road
Port Townsend, WA 98368
(360) 385-3051

Mining Hall
(pp. 186-191)
ARCHITECT/DESIGNER
Bensonwood Homes
BUILDER
RCK Builders, Inc.
P.O. Box 3192
Evergreen, CO 80439
(303) 674-0350
TIMBERFRAMER
Benson Woodworking

In Addition

Master's Wing
(pp. 194-195)
ARCHITECT/DESIGNER
Design Associates
BUILDER
Norm Abram
TIMBERFRAMER
Benson Woodworking

Abundant Farm
(pp. 196-197)
ARCHITECT/DESIGNER
Steven Hale Associates
12 Everett Road
Jamaica Plains, MA 02130
(617) 522-9999
BUILDER
Robert Kennedy
New Boston, MA
TIMBERFRAMER
Benson Woodworking

Trumpet Haven
(pp. 198-199)
ARCHITECT/DESIGNER
Hollis-Crocker Architects P.C.
BUILDER
Daniel Owens Construction
25 Dug Hill Road
Landrum, SC 29356
(864) 457-4305
TIMBERFRAMER
Benson Woodworking

Barn Anew
(pp. 200-201)
ARCHITECT/DESIGNER
Durrant Design
P.O. Box 278
Harvard, MA 01451
(978) 456-3695
BUILDER
T. H. Smith Building and
Remodeling
4 Squareshire Road
Sterling, MA 01564
(978) 365-3611
TIMBERFRAMER
Benson Woodworking

Timber Sanctum
(pp. 202-203)
ARCHITECT/DESIGNER
Bensonwood Homes
BUILDER
Michael Nerrie
RR1, Box 545
Walpole, NH 03608
(603) 756-4179
TIMBERFRAMER
Benson Woodworking

Thatched Nest
(pp. 204-207)
ARCHITECT/DESIGNER
Bensonwood Homes
BUILDER
Beeton and Lennard Ltd.
Shottisham, Woodbridge
Suffolk 1P12 3ET, England
TIMBERFRAMER
Benson Woodworking

*The historical photos on
pp. 16-17, 74-75, 138-139, 192-
193, and 208-209 are courtesy
the Darius Kinsey Collection,
Whatcom Museum of History &
Art, Bellingham, Washington.*

Visit the author's website at:
www.bensonwood.com.